Sioux Center
Sudan

Sioux Center
Sudan

A MISSIONARY NURSE'S JOURNEY

JEFF BARKER

HENDRICKSON PUBLISHERS

Library of Congress Cataloging-in-Publication Data

Names: Barker, Jeff Allen, 1954- author.
Title: Sioux Center Sudan : a farm girl's missionary journey / Jeff Barker.
Description: Peabody, Massachusetts : Hendrickson Publishers, [2018] |
  Includes bibliographical references.
Identifiers: LCCN 2017049210 | ISBN 9781683070856 (alk. paper)
Subjects: LCSH: Schuiteman, Arlene, 1924- | Reformed Church in
  America--Missions--Sudan. | Missionaries, Medical--South
  Sudan--Nasir--Biography. | Nurses--Sudan--Biography. | LCGFT: Biographies.
Classification: LCC R722.32.S34 B37 2018 | DDC 610.6909624--dc23
  LC record available at https://lccn.loc.gov/2017049210

For Daniel,
who loves books and stories
and is a truth-seeker

But this is the one to whom I will look,
to the humble and contrite in spirit,
who trembles at my word.

Isaiah 66:2b (NRSV)

Contents

ACKNOWLEDGMENTS — ix

PROLOGUE — xv

1 DID YOU EVER WANT TO BE A NURSE? — 1

2 THE GLOWING GIRL — 8

3 A TORN TRIANGLE — 15

4 THE REASON WHY I CRY — 23

5 YOU-WILL-BE-GOOD, DAUGHTER-OF-JOHN — 28

6 FISHING DAY — 40

7 SOUTH SUDAN, JULY 1955 — 49

8 NIGHT IN THE VILLAGE — 78

9 I AM A DOG — 87

10 BEGINNINGS — 92

11 WHERE'S THE GOOD? — 97

12 NYAKOTA'S FEET — 102

13 JɔK JAK — 108

14 YUɔL — 114

15 SPENDING THE DAY IN HEAVEN — 126

16 THE FLY — 136

17 THE BOY WHO FELL   142

18 THE UNSCRUPULOUS GOD   154

19 WITH PAINFUL LABOR   162

20 DO YOU KNOW ANY DISCIPLES?   170

21 WE WILL NOT SEE YOUR EYES AGAIN   193

22 THE SOBAT RIVER OVERFLOWS   202

SELECTED BIBLIOGRAPHY   209

PHOTOGRAPHS   213

🌀 Acknowledgments

At the time of this writing, the town of Nasir in the South Sudan has diminished into rubble, the detritus of war. This book tells stories that together reveal the arc of the life of that little town. And one Iowa town. And one woman who loved them both.

When Arlene lived in Nasir, the nation was known as the Sudan, which is how Arlene refers to it in her journals and letters. Now there are two nations, and the map shows that Nasir is in the country known as the South Sudan. This book adheres mostly to the name of the nation as it was in the mid-twentieth century.

The sharing of these stories would not have been possible without, well, so many helpers that it astonishes me to think of it. This is the culmination of a long journey—including Arlene's faithful life of journaling and letter writing—that became plays, songs, and stories, all trying to hint at the larger story of God at work in the world.

Arlene has put countless hours into this years-long project. Her patience, courage, intelligence, wit, and wisdom have been nothing short of a joy to me, enriching my own life beyond measure. Even though I am this book's writer, I should note that some of the best phrases come from Arlene's own writing—words that were crafted in faithfulness at the end of exhausting days. I do not know how she kept up her practice of journaling, but she did. Arlene has been a diarist throughout her adult life. If she had not kept those records, the details would have been lost by the time I met her. Her journals include written prayers, talking to her Maker as friend to friend. In addition, Arlene has been a disciplined letter writer and filer of old letters, both sent and received. These journals, letters, and other papers are a remarkable collection, a glimpse into a unique landscape of the soul, a long journey of faithfulness. Arlene's trust in sharing so many of these materials with me is a gift I will forever cherish.

Arlene introduced me to her friend Eleanor Vandevort, who also is called Vandy, Van, and Nyarial. Vandy's book *A Leopard Tamed* is a treasure, and you should read it for a smart and gripping view into Sudanese culture. By the time I met Vandy, her book was out of print, but thankfully *A Leopard Tamed* is returning to print at the same time as this new book (originally published in 1968 and republished for its fiftieth anniversary in 2018 by Hendrickson, including a new introduction from Elisabeth Elliot's daughter, Valerie Elliot Shepard). Although Vandy has gone to be with the Lord, surely she would throw up her hands in delight to know that her version of the story and her dear friend Arlene's version are being shared side by side.

Vandy was sheer delight. One day I answered the phone, and all I heard was singing. It was Vandy, singing me a song in Nuer. That was the first time I met her! Vandy and Arlene were the closest of friends, and I was privileged to observe that friendship. Vandy read some early chapters of this book, and then we lost her. She died on October 26, 2015. I don't know if there will be books in heaven, but if so, I am eager for Vandy to fact-check me. She will tell the truth, for if anything, Vandy was honest. I loved her for it.

Together, Arlene and I created three short plays that were presented in the United States, Japan, and Ethiopia: *Sioux Center Sudan, Iowa Ethiopia,* and *Zambia Home.* These plays were then collected into a longer (and slightly different) play called *Arlene: An African Trilogy,* which was presented at Northwestern College in Orange City, Iowa, as a celebratory culmination of a decade-long theatrical project. While the plays are a mere foundation to what you now read, all those early helpers in that longer project should be remembered here.

The theatre artists who were part of the earliest Drama Ministries Ensemble productions of the plays walked patiently with Arlene and me through the difficult and sometimes scary journeys of those three world-premiere productions. They are Kristen Olson-Jones Brind, Kristi Woodyard Christenson, Stephen Stonebraker, Margareta DeBoer Maxon, Lois Estell, Tessa Drijfhout-Rosier, Rachel Foulks, Megan Hodgin, Brady Greer Huffman, Matt Hulstein, Tracey Pronk Hulstein, Micah Trapp, Brett Vander Berg, Lindsay Westerkamp Bauer, Hannah Barker Nickolay, Dan Laird, Jackson Nickolay, Dan Sikkema, Kristin Trease, Aleah Stenberg, Shelby Vander Molen, Amalia Vasquez, Huiyu Lin, Tesla McGillivray Kasten, Jacob Christiansen, Brianne Hassman Christiansen, Marisol Seys, Ali Sondreal, Eric Van Der Linden, and Megan Weidner.

Actors in the original production of *Arlene: An African Trilogy* were John Amodeo, Jacob Christiansen, Megan Cole, Christa Curl, Brianne Hassman Christiansen, Amanda Hays, Abby McCubbin, Brody Van Roekel, and Megan Vipond. The wonderful design team included Amber Beyer, Rachel Hanson Starkenburg, Amber Huizenga, Theresa Larrabee, Jana Latchaw, Jackson Nickolay, Jonathan Sabo, Drew Schmidt, and Rowan Sullivan. Tiffany Hach, Alex Wendel, and Logan Wright supported Karen Bohm Barker at the director's table.

Northwestern College Theatre Department secretaries Kelly Van Marel and Jen Sabo, along with student assistants Kristin Trease and Dan Sikkema, have been crucial to this project. Dan's paternal grandparents, Verne and Lorraine, along with Dan's father Milt, were kind enough to spend hours sharing some of their experiences in the Sudan and Ethiopia.

Joonna Trapp, expert teacher of creative nonfiction, provided inspiring and supportive counsel early in the book portion of this project. I think I could not have a better friend and cheerleader than Joonna.

Karen Burton Mains provided feedback on early chapters, and her encouraging imprint has extended to this whole project.

Russell Gasero is a historian for the Reformed Church, and he provided expert and prompt assistance more than once. Greta Grond and Sarah Huyser were two additional library assistants for this project. Donald Bruggink, editor of the Reformed Church in America Historical Series, provided appreciated encouragement and counsel.

Special thanks to some early readers of the book who provided invaluable feedback and encouragement: Grada Kiel, Amy Keahi, Juliana Else, Nancy Franken, Steve Carpenter, Kristin Kroesche, Joanne Barker, and Doris Bohm. My sisters Chris Jackson and Jane Carpenter have cheered their brother on in remarkable ways.

Doug Calsbeek, editor of *Sioux County Capital Democrat*, facilitated a prepublication serialization of portions of the book and gave valuable editing advice throughout the journey of serialization.

Carrie Martin and Patricia Anders of Hendrickson Publishers have been amazing encouragers. Patricia's attention to editing detail has been nothing short of remarkable.

Kim Van Es, my colleague at Northwestern College, is the gracious, good-humored, and wise copy editor of early drafts whose creative and razor-sharp way with words is present in every paragraph. I consider her friendship to the project a true godsend.

Vaughn Donahue was our graphic designer for the prepublication phase of this book. He is a good friend to me personally, as well as a good friend to the project. He has been with the project from the beginning, having designed the beautiful poster for the first play *Sioux Center Sudan* (which is also seen on the cover of this book).

Amanda Kundert, who created hand-drawn charcoal illustrations to accompany many of the stories in this book, has the gift of a great collaborator, always ready to say, "Let's try!"

Other immediate family members have made huge contributions to this project, beyond their general encouragements poured into me. My beloved Karen Bohm Barker has been the project's detailed and faithful literary coach. She's the one who received every first "Listen to this!" and "Here's another chapter." She is a fine writer, teacher, artist, and critic, and I trust her feedback more than anyone else in my life. Daniel James Barker helped by doing valuable cultural research. Composer Joseph Barker wrote a new Ethiopian-style melody as we created *Iowa Ethiopia*. Kay Gillette Barker is an avid reader and passionate performer, and she gave me the wisdom of an objective newcomer early in the process. My son-in-law Jackson Nickolay is a thoughtful, creative, and patient theatre artist, and it was a joy to watch him fall in love with my daughter as they worked on two of the Arlene plays.

Speaking of my daughter, Hannah Barker Nickolay, she poured her heart and heartbreaking talent into enacting Arlene in two of the plays. Eventually, Hannah became the archivist of Arlene's slide collection, working with Arlene along with my colleague Drew Schmidt to create descriptions and post the collection online. That collection may be found at http://portfolios.nwciowa.edu/arlene/default2.aspx. Hannah went a step further by applying her love of language in the crucible of reading early drafts, trying to nudge her father to be a better writer. She is amazing to me. And I wish I were half the poet she is.

There have been so many more friends of this storytelling journey. I'm grateful for each one of them, whether or not their names are mentioned here. But I must stop listing names so we can get on with the story!

Jeff Barker
Orange City, Iowa

 # Prologue

On her nineteenth birthday, Arlene Schuiteman received a gift that would change her life. After church, Grandma Schuiteman slipped Arlene a small, red cardboard box. Inside the box was a lockable, leather-bound book with gold letters on the cover: *Five Year Diary*. The inside title page carried the subtitle *In which should be recorded important events most worthy of remembrance*. A diary with a sense of mission.

Although Arlene received the diary on the third day of January in 1943, she was raised to avoid wastefulness of any kind, so she backtracked two days. In tiny handwriting, she filled in the four lines assigned for January 1:

> *Friday. Grandma Schuiteman's*
> *69th birthday. Went out there in P.M.*
> *Lots of fun. Cold and icy so*
> *we had to stay home at night.*

And four more lines for January 2:

> *Saturday. Washed, ironed,*
> *baked bread, churned, made ice-*
> *cream. Mopped and waxed dining*
> *room after supper. Busy.*

Now caught up to January 3, she wrote in neat cursive with a blue pen:

> *Sun. Happy Birthday. Snow storm in*
> *A.M. Light candles in C.E. Gerrit, Nelvina,*
> *John & I to Rob Remmerde's—fun.*
> *Chocolates from John.*

At Christian Endeavor youth group that Sunday evening, candles were lit in honor of the first meeting of the New Year. After C.E., Arlene and some friends drove out to the Remmerde farm for snacks and games.

A young man named John, a bachelor farmer, who had driven over from Orange City to bring Arlene a birthday present, joined the party. He was the only sweetheart Arlene had known, and she was reserved about it. John's name seldom appeared in Arlene's diary. She was slowly working out what it meant for something in her life to be "most worthy of remembrance."

The entries in her diary placed more importance on the normal rhythms of farm and family than on anything personal. Weather: *6 below in the morning.* Outings: *Went to Morry's Café.* Routines of the farm: *Little pigs came so we can't go to Sioux City Saturday.*

Every so often, her diary revealed an internal struggle: *Didn't study much because trying to make up mind whether to quit John or not.* Two days later: *Came home about 12:10 then I quit John.* The next day, an emotion was recorded: *Feel kinda blue. Didn't sleep much last night. Cleaned closet.*

For those five years, Arlene wrote entries for each day without fail. Her grandmother's gift was honored with completion. Arlene showed her record book to no one. She kept the diary in her undergarment drawer and hid the key. Not that this care was called for. Arlene was of a culture that prized privacy. No one in the Schuiteman household would have peeked if Arlene had left her diary unlocked and lying open on the davenport in the front room.

When she had filled every page, Arlene put the diary back into its red box and carefully stored it in her hope chest. Her parents and sisters knew of her journaling, and they gave her the gift of another five-year diary at the start of 1948. She stopped journaling while in nursing school, but resumed the daily practice the year she moved to Africa, eventually writing longer entries in blank journals. She could fill a book in a single year. A daily practice had been firmly established. Journal after journal was completed. And then put away.

So how did Arlene Schuiteman and her lifetime of journals finally connect with a theatre professor from Northwestern College? The year was 2005, and I was considering writing a play about Betty Greene, a pioneer among female airplane pilots and one of the founders of the Missionary Aviation Fellowship. I learned that an eighty-one-year-old woman living not far from me had known Betty Greene in Africa. When I called to ask her about Betty, she invited me to her home. We sat in her dining room and talked about her. During our second meeting, I told Arlene that my play should not be about Betty Greene—the play should be about Arlene Schuiteman. Would she give me permission?

She answered my question with a condition: I must agree never to put a missionary on a pedestal. I said yes.

Over the next several years, Arlene told me enough of her story that I was able to write a trilogy of plays set in the Sudan, Ethiopia, and Zambia. The plays were performed throughout the United States and then overseas, in Ethiopia and Japan.

During this time, Arlene and I became friends. At some point, she told me she kept diaries. Sometimes she would loan me a diary, if she felt it might help my work, but she always asked me not to show her diaries to anyone.

When she turned ninety, she made a bold decision. She gave me all her diaries. She packed up forty-six years of her life's writings and held the door open so I could carry them out to my car. She included her very first five-year diary and all the personal journals from the years she was in Africa. She told me I could ask her anything about what was in them.

She said, "When you're finished with them, I don't want them back. You decide what to do with them." Arlene had offered me that rarity of rarities—the key to a hidden treasure extended on an open palm.

1

Did You Ever Want to Be a Nurse?

Tues. Rainy and dark. No beginners and no fifth grade. 13 pupils. Tired at night. Went to Mission Fest in Orange City.

August 29, 1944

She almost burst into tears. She knew Dr. Harrison's invitation was for her, but she saw no way to accept it.

Six miles east and six miles south of the Schuiteman farm, the 1944 Orange City Mission Festival was about to have a challenging conclusion. The annual conference was an opportunity for rural Iowa Christians to learn firsthand about the church's work around the world. The festival speakers told personal stories of exotic lands far away, similar to the travelogue presenters who were popular in that era. In the case of missionary speakers, however, there was the possibility of personal participation in the stories being shared. Listeners were encouraged to pray, write letters, and contribute financially. They could also join one of the area's "Mission Bands"—groups that prepared barrels of used shirts and shoes (items outgrown with no one to hand down to), soap, toothpaste, socks, blankets, and old sheets torn into strips to be used as bandages. Churches put missions in their budgets, and individuals gave sacrificially. Foreign missions were important in the northwest Iowa of Arlene Schuiteman's upbringing.

The Mission Festival speakers always issued an invitation to consider leaving Iowa behind. Listeners were asked if they should and would travel to a foreign land to become a missionary. Arlene was in attendance at the 1944 event with her mother and five sisters (most of the attendees that year were women). Three years earlier, just before Christmas of 1941, the citizens of Sioux County had huddled at their radios to hear President Roosevelt describe the date that would "live in infamy." Now, three years later, northwest Iowa's young men were still off at war.

Arlene's father, Pa as he was called, had stayed home that night to do the farm chores. Johanna Schuiteman and her six daughters arrived early, as they always did. They were able to park close to the entrance of the Orange City Town Hall on that wet Tuesday. The two-story, tan brick building looked a bit like a military Quonset hut with its curved top and undecorated facade. A wide exterior staircase led from the sidewalk to a second-story multipurpose room typical of that era's auditoriums—a space useful for ball games, concerts, plays, and community events.

Her mother, Ma Schuiteman, and Ma's line of girls quickly climbed the stairs, went inside, crossed the varnished hardwood floor, and found folding chairs close (but not too close) to the front of the stage. Latecomers would have to sit on the bleachers in the back.

Ma had changed out of the cotton dress she typically wore for a whole week before washing it. Tonight was an occasion for her Sunday best. Very few moments in the course of a week caused Ma to set her apron aside, but the Mission Festival was definitely one of them. Ma was a short woman, skinny, with long brown hair that she would rebraid each night. Most of the women of Ma's generation kept their hair long throughout their lives. One of Ma's few audacious acts in her life was the day she surprised everyone at the farm by coming back from town with her hair cut short and curled. But that was down the road. Tonight Ma's hair was long and braided.

All seven Schuiteman women wore dresses Ma had made. Ma was an excellent seamstress: she could look at a catalog picture and create a pattern for tucks, yokes, skirts, and pleats. She could make anything the girls asked. She bought good material and chose excellent colors.

Arlene stood out as the tallest of the daughters. She was thin, with short brown hair, and her hands were large and strong. She moved with purpose, and when she stood, she was straight as a post. At twenty years of age, Arlene had a strong set of core values inherited from her family and church. She had publicly professed her Christian faith and was a practitioner of its disciplines. She believed Jesus taught her to love everyone everywhere. She was intelligent and curious. She had a deep sense of responsibility. She knew that people expected much of her, and she tried to do the right thing, no matter the difficulty.

Arlene's life trajectory already seemed set. She had a high school diploma and an elementary school teaching certificate. She loved children, and she loved farm life. It seemed most likely that someday she would become a farmer's wife. One year earlier, she had a special beau. She quit that relationship when Ma expressed concern about the man's family. The opinion of Arlene's parents was a paramount value in her life.

Now, on an August night in the Orange City Town Hall, a new trajectory would present itself for Arlene's consideration. Her age, smarts, farm-bred skills, and personal faith made her an extremely suitable candidate for the mission field. She had not previously given serious thought to just how suited she was.

Tonight's speaker had faced the dangers of wartime travel across the ocean to come here to ask someone (he didn't know whom) to pack up and move across the world. Though needs were great in northwest Iowa, the speaker would argue that some needs were greater elsewhere.

The medical missionary who had come from the Middle East to Orange City was Dr. Paul Harrison. Although he was close to retirement, his handsomeness belied his age: he carried his square jaw with forthrightness, had been a Johns Hopkins honors gradu-ate, and spoke Arabic fluently. Dr. Harrison had served his entire missionary career, spanning two world wars, in the Arabian Peninsula, mostly in Oman and Bahrain. He became so famous in Oman that, to this day, if you walk the streets of the seaside capital, Muscat, and ask the locals if they have heard of Dr. Paul Harrison, they are likely to respond with reverence and gratitude. Few would be old enough to have met him, but his name is like that of a classic movie star. Omani people know that their lives are better because a Christian doctor came and lived in their desert land. For years, Harrison was the only doctor in Oman. He made house calls on camelback and founded Muscat's hospital. Now in his sixties, Dr. Harrison had a full head of hair, tightly cropped. When preaching or speaking, he wore thick, black-rimmed glasses and a baggy suit. He was most at home in the operating room or traveling house to house in desert climes. But on this rainy Tuesday in August, he made his way onto a small town stage to unabashedly issue a call for help.

Most of the women at the conference had thought about the question, "Will you become a missionary?" For various reasons, they had set the question aside: they had already chosen their life's occupation, or they were waiting for something else—waiting to attend college, waiting for someone to come home from the war, waiting for rationing to be lifted, waiting to have money again, and so on.

Harrison declared, "The most crucial need now in Arabia is nurses. We need nurses. We are praying that the Lord will provide nurses. That is our prayer in this most desperate hour."

Arlene scarcely moved or even breathed. She realized now she had been waiting for this night.

Harrison asked, "Did you ever want to be a nurse?"

Arlene was not at all surprised at her inner answer: Yes, she did. She had wanted to be a nurse for as long as she could remember.

"Do you have the work ethic for the training?"

She was not John G. Schuiteman's daughter for nothing.

"Is God calling you? Will you say yes?"

She wanted very much to say yes, but how could she? She had already invested two years in the Normal Training Course so she could be credentialed to teach. Now she had a teaching contract, and her career as an educator was just beginning.

Each morning, the three elder Schuiteman sisters—Harriet, Arlene, and Bernice—left the farm together in the well-worn Model A Ford that Pa had purchased for his daughters to drive to their teaching jobs. The sisters taught at three separate country schools in which grades one through eight all learned together in a single room.

The sisters' teaching days were divided into segments, during which students of a particular grade had their lessons with the teacher while students of the other grades did their homework. The school days also contained chores, like fetching water from a neighboring farm, cleaning the chalkboard, dusting out the erasers, sweeping the floor, and stoking the fire. Sometimes during those war years, lessons would be called off for a day while teachers led their students on walks to collect milkweed pods for the manufacture of parachute silk.

Country schools were situated two miles apart, making it possible for children to get to their school by walking a mile or so. Arlene drove the Model A since her school was farthest out. She first drove straight north to Harriet's school, which sat on the far side of Plantage's farm. After dropping off Harriet, Arlene turned west on 340th Street. Her sister Bernice's school was next, a mile north of the tiny town of Carmel. Then two more miles brought Arlene to her own school, Plato Township School #2, on the northwest corner of 340th and Fig Avenue.

The roads were not graveled yet, and Arlene learned to navigate muddy ruts with the Model A. She used her horn plenty to alert the children walking the country roads to school. Once when she and her sisters were driving past the Plantage farm, a roll of barbed wire blew into their path. The wire caught the wheel, yanking the car into the ditch. Mr. Plantage came running out to untangle the wire, and then he used his horse team to pull the car out of the ditch. All was well in a short time. There were no lawsuits or insurance claims, and everyone went about their business.

In the evenings, Arlene backtracked, picking up her sisters before they all headed home to do the farm chores, mark papers, prepare lessons, and get ready to do it all over again.

School days were a ballet on the Schuiteman farm. Bright and early, two of the girls went outside to feed the cows, horses, and chickens, while the other girls tended to the lunch buckets. They sliced bread for sandwiches, put cake or pie into containers, and included a raw potato for tossing into the hot ashes at the base of the coal-burning furnace at school—by lunchtime, the potato would be baked and ready. Teachers and students all brought packed lunches. Each bucket included butter and salt for the potato, as well as a thermos of soup or hot chocolate.

Country schoolteachers knew all their students' families, visiting their students' farms as part of their duties, sometimes staying overnight. Very often, the teachers were simply visiting relatives, since extended families tended to homestead close together for safety and to help one another with harvesting.

This was a family world, a tribal world. One person's stability grounded the stability of others. A stable woman of that era typically chose one of three occupations: teacher, secretary, or nurse. When a woman landed one of those jobs, she kept it. Or she got married.

The three elder Schuiteman sisters were presently single and employed.

Arlene's parents had not raised her to be wasteful or impulsive. She was not a quitter, and she knew that the decisions of individual members of the clan impacted everyone. A change in one cog would change the whole wheel.

She had wanted to say yes on that last night of the Mission Festival, but how could she?

Arlene had heard Pa say that after the war they could get a refrigerator, but now was not the time to be making a big change. Arlene reasoned that this was also not the time to be quitting a perfectly good teaching job. She had responsibilities on the farm, at school, and at the church. The call had come at a bad time. She would wait.

After joining their voices in the closing hymn of the Mission Festival of 1944, the seven Schuiteman women squeezed into their car and drove the twelve miles home. Arlene went upstairs to her bedroom, folded up the call to missionary nursing, and packed it away. She got up the next morning and drove to Plato #2. That night she wrote in her journal, "Lot of school work." So it would be for seven more years.

2

The Glowing Girl

*Sunday. Home in A.M. Made dinner. To
church in P.M. Taught S.S. To C.E. Bernice to
Grandma S. Telephone lines out of order.*

March 4, 1951

Then came the Sunday that would stand out from every other
Sunday in Arlene's young life.

Much of the prior week was already in the running for memo-
rability. First of all, Arlene had a terrible toothache, and the dentist tried everything short of pulling the tooth. Then the weather
turned gray. On Friday morning, Arlene and her students made it
to the schoolhouse as usual. An hour later, March roared in like a
lion. By midmorning, Arlene called it a day and bundled her students homeward for fear they might get trapped in the school that
weekend. This turned out to be a good decision. Snow fell all that
day, through the night, and all day Saturday.

Northwest Iowa churches rarely cancelled Sunday services.
These Christians were Sabbatarian and held the Lord's Day in high
esteem. The other days of the week either led to or trailed from
what they considered the most important day, the day of the fourth
commandment: "Remember the Sabbath day to keep it holy." Keeping the Sabbath holy included gathering at the church building for
corporate worship, but it seemed that worship services might be
cancelled this particular weekend.

On Saturday night, Pa went out to clear some of the snow in
preparation for Sunday. Pa always did everything early. To never be
late was one of his life values. Consequently, he was always running.

He ran from the house to the barn and the hog lot to the calf pen. He was not a jogger for sport, but he loved to be moving quickly. He taught his girls to get their work done early and never be late.

Tardiness was a sin to Pa. In earlier days, when he drove the girls to Welcome #4, the country school at the intersection a mile north of the farm, they once arrived one minute late. Pa told the girls to wait in the car while he went inside to speak to the teacher.

"Are my girls late?"

"One minute."

"Are you going to count them tardy?"

"Well, I don't think so, since it's only one minute."

"Then I'll send them in. If they were going to get marked tardy, I was taking them home."

"Why?"

"Better to get marked absent."

Pa's ethos was based upon frugality. Nothing was to be wasted, and that included time. Minutes and seconds were valuable. Pa valued his own time as well as everyone else's. One must not keep someone waiting. Slowness was a cousin of sloth, one of the seven deadly sins.

Pa was a man who knew what he wanted, and he was disciplined enough to get it. His daughters could count on him, and they developed great love and respect for him. He was taller than Arlene, he had a ruddy complexion, and his thick, black hair eventually grayed a bit but never fell out. Like farmers everywhere, Pa wore a cap that shielded his eyes from the sun. By 1951, Pa was farming with a tractor, but he still used horses for many of his tasks. Horse farming was in his blood. He no longer used horse teams for the most difficult chores, like the first plowing of spring. But for chores like mowing and raking, he would rather be rolling with reins in his hands, listening to the rattle of the doubletree, the clatter of the long blades sliding back and forth, the thump of Sam's and Jewell's feet in the sod, and the huffs of breath coming from their nostrils. The smell was not the sting of diesel overwhelming everything natural, but the sweat of the horses commingled with alfalfa, which was, to Pa, the sweetest smell in the world.

Whether Pa was holding a tractor steering wheel or his team's reins, he was seated in the open sunshine. Because he wore a cap, his forehead was always in the shade and never tanned like the lower half of his face. On Sundays when farmers took off their caps, one could easily glance across the pews at First Reformed Church and pick out the farmers by their two-toned visages.

On that white-covered Sunday of March 4, 1951, the day dawned bright and clear with no new precipitation. There would be church. Pa rushed out to clear the remaining snow. Two of the girls eventually joined Pa to do the milking and feed the animals.

Inside the house, Ma sifted together the dry ingredients for the pancake batter and said to the girls meandering into the kitchen, "One of you get the eggs." She did not mean just any eggs. She meant the cracked eggs. Uncracked eggs were placed carefully into flats to trade for groceries at Balkema's. Cracked eggs were for home use. Morning cracked eggs were for pancakes or sometimes French toast. When the outside crew came in from the chores, they all sat down.

By 8:30, Ma and Pa were up from the table, and by 9:00, they were driving out of the farmyard, heading for the early service. The girls always skipped the morning service, staying home to do the breakfast dishes and fix Sunday dinner. Another reason the girls stayed home during the early service was that throughout their growing up years, the 9:30 service had been in Dutch.

During World War I, however, there had been an exception. Iowa's Governor Harding had issued an executive order that public communication must be in English, including church services, funerals, sidewalk conversations, and even telephone talk if it was a party line. During the war, Iowa had been the only state to take an official action against non-English languages. The reasons were complex, but a fear of "outsiders" was behind the governor's action. Sioux Center and many other Iowa towns were full of immigrants who treasured their native language. They taught it to their children and grandchildren. Most especially, they kept it as their preferred language for prayer and in speaking about God. Arlene's own Grandma Rozeboom offered special treats to her granddaughters if they could recite a Bible passage in the Dutch of the old country. But language is dependent on usage, and during Arlene's formative years, church became pretty much the only public arena in which Dutch was regularly heard. Eventually the churches adjusted, and the second service (the afternoon service) was practiced in English.

In 1948, the Sioux Center First Reformed Church called a new pastor who did not speak Dutch. On April 25 of that year, the final service in Dutch was held. Ma and Pa continued to attend both services since their parents attended the early service, and they were not about to change. All the generations had their routines, and routines changed slowly in northwest Iowa.

Shortly before noon on March 4, 1951, Ma and Pa arrived home from attending the first service. The girls had laid out Sunday dinner in the cozy farmhouse kitchen. The family all settled into their places around a Formica table with metal legs and an oilcloth covering. There was a formal table in the dining room, but that was reserved for guests and special occasions. The kitchen was the room of choice when it was just the eight of them. Close proximity was a blessing, never a hardship.

The girls finished their meals, but no one left the table. At the right time, Pa caught the eye of his eldest daughter and whispered, "Get the book." Getting "the book" was a privilege all the girls cherished. Today was Harriet's turn. She quickly retrieved it from its special shelf in the large cupboard that stood against the north

wall. She then handed the book to Pa. The same routine had occurred that morning after breakfast, and the same routine would
occur that evening after supper. Find the crocheted bookmark, find
the verse they had last read, and read another chapter from the
Holy Bible.

Pa would sometimes stop reading to quiz one of the girls about
a verse. This was his playful way of making sure they were paying
attention. He sometimes handed the book to one of the girls and
asked that daughter to finish the reading. She would hold the sa-
cred book in her hands with a sense of privilege, taking care not to
let it touch her plate. She would read until Pa said, "All right," and
she would hand the book back to him. He replaced the bookmark.
Then the chosen daughter returned the book to its special shelf and
resumed her seat. They were not finished yet. All bowed their heads.
They sat there at the table, praying in silence until finally Ma said,
"Amen." Same routine, seven days a week, morning, noon, and night.

Since today's routine was after Sunday dinner, there was a bit
more urgency. Church was starting again at 1:30. They hurried to
wash the dishes, put away the leftovers, and throw out the scraps for
the dog and cats. Then they dressed, brushed, and powdered. They
had a system for all eight of them to squeeze into the car (some
seated on the forward edge of the seats, some pressed back), trying
not to wrinkle their Sunday best during the short ride to town for
the afternoon service.

The First Reformed Church's building had been erected in 1882,
enlarged in 1884, and ripped down by a tornado in 1902. The determined church members immediately put up a brick building—a
grand edifice with a tall bell tower. That building was still their
worship center in 1951. The services, like the building itself, were
generally solemn. "Let all things be done decently and in order"
(1 Corinthians 14:40) was the biblical text that shaped the worship
ethos of the congregations of the Reformed Churches in America.

In some of the local Reformed churches, the organist and choir
were situated behind the congregation so as not to draw attention

to themselves or create any sense of performance. This was not the case in Arlene's home church, where the choir loft and organ console were at the front. Choral anthems, soloists, and quartets were much appreciated, although a certain quiet decorum prevailed. The choir never swayed when they sang. No hands were raised. There was no speaking in tongues so, obviously, no interpretation of tongues. King David would have had second thoughts about dancing at First Reformed Church in Sioux Center, Iowa.

Ma and Pa found their usual pew on the main floor and sat there with the younger girls (Grada, Joyce, and Milly). The older girls (Harriet, Arlene, and Bernice) took the stairs up to the gallery that hovered over and wrapped around the sanctuary like the forecastle of a great ship. There the Schuiteman sisters sat with the members of Christian Endeavor, a group of a hundred or so young adults. Arlene was the current C.E. president.

Many of the young adults in the gallery that Sunday were up there doing what young adults do. Some were already seated next to their dates for later that evening, while others were considering who they wanted to ask out or be asked by. The gallery was a place for religious observance, but it was also a sort of social club for young, single Christians.

During that Sunday's sermon, however, one young woman was thinking nothing at all about social opportunities. She was listening carefully. She had already observed that Reverend P. A. De Jong was a God-seeker. She could see that the Christian way and its call on his life were very real to him. He did not lead the church like a business as some other pastors did. This pastor was a gospel man.

That day, Reverend De Jong preached from the prophecy of Isaiah, chapter 6. King Uzziah was dead, so change was in the wind for the people of Judah. Isaiah had a vision—a flight of angels with six wings each. The angels sang, "The whole earth is full of God's glory!" The building shook. A fiery altar spilled smoke everywhere. Isaiah was terrified. The voice of the Lord was heard to say, "Whom shall I send? And who will go for us?"

Looking up from his Bible, Reverend De Jong repeated the question to his own congregation: "Who will we send?"

He meant it not as a rhetorical question but as an actual question. His church was an evangelical church that supported missionaries around the world. They believed that the gospel story was, indeed, good news and that when Jesus told his followers to carry his story to the ends of the earth, he meant everywhere. Arlene's home church took their assignment seriously.

"Who will *we* send? Who will go for *us*?"

What happened next was a supernatural event for which Arlene has no proof or witnesses, but to her it was real.

With her pastor's words echoing in her ears, Arlene glanced down at her arms, then at her hands, her legs, her feet. She looked. She stared. She was glowing! She felt hot—heat coursing through her body. Astounded, she looked around, expecting everyone to be glowing. But no one else was. She was the only one. Now she was embarrassed, because she was about to attract considerable attention—a distress to someone of her personality. She started to slump down, trying to disappear. She glanced around again, but no one was looking at her. One boy was sleeping. No one had noticed. Only she could tell this was happening. This was just for her, only her. The sensation did not subside quickly. It persisted many minutes. A connection surged from testament to testament, Isaiah 6 to Acts 2, then from Pentecost's upper room to that Sioux Center church gallery on a wintery Sunday afternoon. A nonconsuming fire. The Holy Spirit of God.

She sat up and whispered, "Here am I. Send me."

3

A Torn Triangle

*Saturday. Terrible icy. Joyce and I got
haircuts. Milly a Toni by Gert. Did work
in P.M. Went to Rev. De Jong in A.M.*

March 10, 1951

The glow subsided. The afternoon service ended. Arlene's duties teaching children's Sunday school gave her an excuse to quickly leave the balcony. After class, she walked up the street to Grandma Schuiteman's house where the extended family was having coffee and cake as they did every Sunday after the second service. Around four o'clock, same as every week, one of the men stood up and announced time for chores, and the gathering disbanded. Arlene and her parents and sisters packed into the Schuitemans' good car, a Pontiac, for the four-mile trek back to the farm. Pa finished the second milking of the day. Ma and the girls set the table and made supper. Supper included fried eggs and fried potatoes that Sunday, every Sunday, nearly every day for that matter. They used that morning's remaining cracked eggs and the leftover boiled potatoes from the noon meal, which they sliced and fried. This routine was a remnant of the frugality brought from the old country, as well as an extension of habits developed during the Great Depression of the 1930s and the war years of the 1940s. Old habits die hard, if at all. But there was a silver lining in the routine—if there were enough cracked eggs, Ma made an angel food cake.

The Schuiteman family ate together almost every morning and night. These mealtimes shaped the overall rhythm of Arlene's childhood—pastoral, joyful, secure, together. Although Arlene sat there at supper that evening, her mind was elsewhere. It was in the church building, up in the gallery, looking down at her glowing skin. She was already in an internal struggle. Who should she tell? Ma? Arlene was not in the habit of keeping any secrets from her mother. Yes, she would tell Ma, but when? Arlene sought a serious conversation on the long-term implications of her supernatural experience. What about next Saturday? Ma would be busy all week maintaining the rhythms of the farm. Monday was wash day. Tuesday was ironing day. Wednesday was bread day. Thursday was everything else day. Friday was baking day. Arlene would likewise be busy with school responsibilities. But Saturday would come, and Arlene would do what she did every Saturday: fix her mother's hair. Each week, Ma's momentum was stopped by the needs of her hair. Ma would finally sit still, and she would look at Arlene in the mirror and ask, "What are you thinking, Arlene?" Arlene looked forward to these times of special intimacy.

Arlene imagined what she might say next Saturday when that exchange occurred.

"What are you thinking, Arlene?"

"Nothing."

"Doesn't seem like nothing."

"Something's happened."

"What?"

"I'm not sure I should talk about it."

"All right. As long as you're *goed* [good]."

"It was last Sunday afternoon. During Reverend De Jong's sermon."

"Oh."

"He asked, 'Who will go for us?'"

"From Isaiah."

"Yes. And I knew what my answer should be. I've been waiting for that question. I know I'm not worthy. It should be someone else . . . someone not so shy . . . someone who's traveled the world . . . someone who's married . . . someone who can speak in public. But

I stopped looking at Reverend De Jong. And I looked down. And my skin was glowing."

"What do you mean?"

"It was really glowing."

"Did anyone else see it?"

"I don't think they could."

"What do you think it meant?"

"That I should say yes. That I should go."

"Go where?"

"Wherever God sends me."

"Away from here?"

"I guess. I guess that's . . . yes."

"Don't you think you can serve God with your life right here in Sioux County?"

There it was. Arlene needed to be able to answer that question. Arlene knew that her mother believed God could and would call her to serve him. She imagined the hopes and fears Ma carried in her prayers for her daughters: "Lord, please call my girls to serve you, but Lord, please don't call them too far away." Arlene believed in her heart that her mother would do everything she could to keep her girls close. Arlene would never want to disobey or disappoint her mother, but neither would she put Ma in a position to make this decision for her. It was not Ma's decision to make. Arlene decided not to tell Ma. Not yet.

If she told her sisters, it would get back to Ma. She would not tell her sisters.

What about Pa? Pa would be proud of her and support her, no matter what. But when Pa found out she was leaving, not just the farm but the United States, his heart would be broken. Such a devastation could be, should be put off as long as possible. No, she would not tell Pa.

Who could she safely tell? Could she carry this secret alone?

The Sunday evening routine continued. Supper ended. Pa asked for the Bible to be brought, and Scripture was read. The family prayed in silence. The older girls headed back to the church for Christian Endeavor. Bernice had recently married, but she was home for the weekend and went to see Grandma Schuiteman.

After Christian Endeavor, Arlene came straight home. She needed time to think. She needed an advisor, but it must be someone who would take her strange experience seriously. If the glowing was of God, then she wanted to respond as her exemplars had. She wondered what Esther or Samuel would tell her—Abraham or Sarah, Deborah or Ruth. She needed help.

By late evening, Arlene had decided there was only one person she could tell. She knew no one more discerning in matters of the Spirit than her pastor, but she wanted to tell him in person and privately. She picked up the phone to make an appointment. The weekend's heavy snow sat on the telephone lines—the phone was dead. She would try again on Monday.

Monday brought warmer weather. Arlene taught school, and then she and the rest of the Mission Band served at a banquet. The rest of the week filled with after-school and evening activities. Tuesday was basketball. Wednesday was visiting relatives. Thursday was her parents' thirtieth wedding anniversary. On Friday, Arlene and some girlfriends went to hear a college chorale from St. Paul sing in Orange City. The week was busy and tiring. Saturday dawned with icy roads, and Arlene awoke with a cold. But she had not forgotten last Sunday's experience nor her intention to speak with her pastor.

Arlene put her two youngest sisters into the Pontiac and white-knuckled the roads into town. The three girls stopped first at the Ida Mulder Beauty Shop. Milly waited while Arlene and Joyce got their cuts. Then Arlene dropped her sisters at Gert's house so Gert could give Milly a perm. Arlene said she would be back but did not say where she was going. This was an easy ruse, since running a list of errands while in town was always expected. Joyce was more than willing to sit and chatter to Milly while the curls set. Arlene went straight to Reverend De Jong's study.

The pastor's study was in the church parsonage. Churches of that era commonly provided housing for preachers and their families in a home called the parsonage, which was usually next door to the church building. This arrangement had advantages for both pastors and churches. Pastors received a residence along with their salary, and church members had twenty-four-hour-a-day access to the pastor.

Arlene parked on the street and stepped briskly up the porch steps, as her Pa would have. She opened the front door without knocking, turned left, and climbed the stairs. At the top of the stairs, she arrived in front of a heavy, oak door. She caught her breath and tapped. Immediately, she heard her pastor's familiar voice saying, "Come in." She entered the tiny, almost claustrophobic office and closed the door behind her.

Reverend De Jong was a bulky man of average height. By the time he accepted the call to First Reformed of Sioux Center, he was balding. He had a gentle but serious gaze from behind rimless glasses. He was very prim, and even though his office was in his home, he wore a tie to work and had his suit jacket on a nearby coat tree.

Reverend De Jong rose and greeted Arlene warmly, making a place for her to sit. He knew her to be a supportive, positive influence in several church groups, and he was always glad to see her.

Arlene had no time to waste and within moments had blurted out her outlandish tale. Her pastor listened carefully and then spoke.

"Glowing?"

"Yes."

"As in really glowing?"

"Yes."

"What do you think it means?"

"That your sermon was meant for me."

"What do you think you should do?"

"That's what I came to you for. What do you think I should do?"

"Arlene. God's will is not difficult to figure out. The difficult thing is to do it."

"I think God wants to send me. I felt the call to missionary nursing seven years ago at the Mission Fest. The timing didn't seem right. Now I think it's time to say yes. How should I do that?"

Reverend De Jong reached behind him and tore off the flap of an envelope. It held a return address, which he handed to her. "Write to that woman. See what she has to say."

The address read, *Miss Ruth Ransom, 156 Fifth Ave, New York, N.Y.* It was the office of the Board of Foreign Missions of the Reformed Church in America.

Arlene left the pastor's study with that address on a torn triangle of paper.

If anything, Arlene was a planner, and as she walked down the stairs, she was already considering what might happen if she wrote a letter to Miss Ransom. Arlene would leave her job . . . leave the farm . . . leave her home church and hometown . . . leave Sioux County . . . leave Iowa. She might go to a place of need on the American continent, such as Appalachian Kentucky, where her Aunt Minn had been a teacher. This address, however, was for *foreign* missions. This step was serious. She might go overseas. If so, there would be no phone calls home except in times of great emergency, if even then. Her mother and father and sisters would go years without hearing her voice, or she theirs. The world was unspeakably large, and she could be lost in it.

She immediately wrote the letter, being quite frank with Miss Ransom:

I have been teaching rural school for eight years and now feel that I wish to give up this work and do some type of missionary work. For several years I've had the feeling that God wanted to use me elsewhere. Since I was a child I've always wanted to be a nurse. My parents advised me to be a teacher. I am 27 years old.

She intended to send the letter in Monday's mail.

Snow fell again Sunday afternoon, and Christian Endeavor was cancelled. By Monday morning, the roads were impassible. Schools were closed. The postman stayed home too. Tuesday was also a snow day. But Arlene had set her jaw about that letter.

Wednesday was finally clear, and Pa used the horses to pull the car over to the highway. School was still cancelled, but the family needed to purchase meat in town—and Arlene needed to mail a letter. Later that same day, Bill Sandbulte stopped by the farm to offer Arlene a new job teaching at the Carmel school. It was a two-room school, with more students and greater responsibility. She said that she would think about his offer and that she needed some time. She didn't tell Bill, but her letter to New York was already at the post office. She would wait for an answer from Miss Ransom before responding about this new teaching opportunity.

Storms resumed on Thursday and continued for the rest of the week. Sunday services were cancelled that weekend. Arlene kept silent on the matter of missions. By the middle of Holy Week, Pa was able to get Arlene to school on a sleigh pulled by the horses. Only five students joined her at the schoolhouse. Arlene's cold that had started the previous week was still with her, and her toothache returned with a vengeance, resulting in an emergency visit to the dentist on Saturday evening. He finally just pulled the tooth. The next day was Easter, and Arlene got up in the dark to attend the sunrise service.

The following week, the roads were all clear, postal service resumed, and a letter arrived from Ruth Ransom. She thanked Arlene for the letter, but they preferred applicants who were much younger. Ransom wrote:

There are many more openings for nurses than teachers. However, when I think you would be at least thirty years old before you could make application to become a missionary, I wonder if that is the thing you should do. . . . In most of the countries, it takes a year and a half or two years to learn the language, so before you could really get your work started you would be almost thirty-three.

Arlene could not help but wonder if she had missed her call seven years earlier. Discouraged but not dissuaded, Arlene postponed responding to any teaching contract for the following year. She quietly filled out applications to nurse training schools. If she wasn't accepted, then she would take the rejections as an indication that she may have misunderstood the call.

Arlene was accepted to not one nursing school, but two.

4

The Reason Why I Cry

You'll go far with your brains and swell personality.
Why someday you may even be Supervisor of
Nurses here—wish you were now—wouldn't
have to put up with "Ripples." Lotza Love.

> Leola Thelen, a fellow student, writing in Arlene's copy
> of The Lamplight, *the 1953 yearbook of the Methodist*
> *Hospital School of Nursing, Sioux City, Iowa*

Arlene kept her own counsel. She told her parents only that she had decided to pursue her childhood dream of becoming a nurse. Her mother was not all that pleased, but Pa was delighted. That fall she moved from the farm into the dorm at Methodist Hospital School of Nursing in Sioux City, Iowa.

She quickly gained the respect of her fellow students as well as her teachers. Her class voted her president. Two years flew by. For the first time in nearly ten years, her personal diary began to collect empty pages.

In Arlene's third and final year of training, Miss Wave Arnold, the supervisor of nurses, made an incredible offer. She told Arlene that if she would go on to the University of Iowa and finish her Bachelor of Science degree, a job as a nursing instructor would await her. The Methodist school would even help her with the cost of tuition.

Before answering, Arlene wrote again to the Board of Foreign Missions, stating directly, "If you think I should not consider missionary nursing, kindly inform me." The secretary quickly wrote back that Ruth Ransom was out of the country and could not be reached, but she sent Arlene a personal information form to start the application process. Arlene straightaway gave her answer to the supervisor of nurses, "Thank you, but no. I have something else to see about first."

Arlene turned down a handful of sure things in favor of uncertainty, decisions based on a belief that God had called her to missions. She was frustrated and lonely. She was also mature enough to agree with the biblical writer to the Hebrews that the nature of faith is an element of uncertainty: "Faith is the substance of things hoped for, the evidence of things not seen" (Hebrews 11:1).

Even though she had no offer in her hand, she prepared to face her greatest obstacle: her family.

In December 1953, her last year of nurses training, an opportunity presented itself to talk with her family on Christmas Day, when they would all be together. This holiday gathering was different from when the girls were younger. Back then, the family celebration was not on December 25 but rather December 6, the Dutch holiday of Sinterklaas Day.

On Sinterklaas Eve, Ma would say to the girls, "I wonder if he'll come tonight." The girls would put a pan of oats out in the yard for Sinterklaas' horse. Then they would sit by the window, looking out into the dark. There was no electric light in the yard, so the only possibility to see him would be if there was an unclouded moon. "Maybe he won't come," Ma would say, but the girls knew differently, and they would stay by the window. Eventually, Pa would say, "Well, I've got to check something in the barn." He always missed getting to see Sinterklaas! Soon after Pa went out, a horse and rider appeared. The rider wore a long coat, and his face was covered with a scarf. He rode his horse up to the pan of oats and dropped some brown paper bags into the snow. Then he was off as quickly as he had come. The girls grabbed their coats and dashed out to gather the bags. There were always just enough bags for each girl, as if Sinterklaas knew who lived there. Each bag contained the same collection of treats: an apple, a large popcorn ball, double-decker fudge, and Christmas holiday candy, which was the girls' favorite—a treat made of rolled dates, figs, coconut, and nuts.

The Decembers of their childhood included special programs at school and church. The children always received candy from their grade school and Sunday school teachers, but no Christmas presents appeared at home. Arlene and her sisters grew up in the wake of the Great Depression, which was framed by the end of one world war and the start of another. Grandpa Rozeboom always gave Arlene's family a bushel of apples at Christmas, which the family treasured, portioning them out with care. December 25 was a religious remembrance, and that was that.

Eventually, an artificial tree was purchased for Christmas on the farm, and the family members drew names so that each person gave and received one gift. This tradition was the one the family practiced when Christmas of 1953 came around. Sinterklaas no longer visited the farm, but Ma still made the holiday candy and special meal for the expanding Schuiteman tribe.

December 25, 1953, fell on a Friday. All six sisters made it out to the farm that night—including Arlene's two married sisters, Harriet and Bernice, with their husbands and three little children. Arlene would be able to tell her whole family at the same time. The house was full, the food was good, Pa was in his prime as a welcoming host, secret names were finally revealed, and gifts were opened. Unbeknownst to those in the room, there was one more secret. Arlene was about to speak when Joyce and her boyfriend Wilmer stole the moment by announcing their engagement. There was much rejoicing, and Arlene held back.

Finally, someone said they had better be getting home. Christmas was about to be over.

"Everybody, before we . . . before you go . . . I was . . . I wanted to . . . I . . . to tell you something." Arlene let the room fill up with silence. She had been waiting almost three years. She did not feel like rushing now.

Pa started to get worried and tried to lighten the air. "Now, what else is coming?"

Arlene took a breath. "What I need to tell you is that . . . I'm going to be a missionary."

No one spoke at first. Then Pa broke the silence. "You're what?"

"I'm going to be a missionary. Probably far away. I've begun the application process. And I wanted everyone to know."

More silence.

Ma said, "We'd better get these little ones bundled up."

That was it. The party broke up, and no one said a word that night about what Arlene had revealed.

The next morning, Pa was already up when Arlene came downstairs.

Longing to hear someone say something, Arlene asked, "How'd you sleep, Pa?"

"I didn't."

"Didn't sleep well?"

"Didn't sleep at all."

"Over what I said?"

"What was the nursing all about?"

"Remember the Mission Fest in Orange City when Dr. Harrison made a call for nurses?"

"I wasn't there."

"You always said I'd make a good nurse. Sometimes I'm slow, but God didn't forget about me."

"So these past three years of nurses training . . ."

"Yeah, Pa."

"A missionary nurse."

"That's right, Pa."

"Achhh. How's that gonna go? You could be gone for years. We got a new hospital right here. They're looking for nurses like mad.

Mijn lieve meisje [My little sweetheart]. God can use nurses right here in Sioux Center."

"I know. That's not my assignment."

"How can you be so sure?"

"How can *you* be so sure?"

Silence.

"Well. You got my heart hitched to two buggies, girl."

"I'm asking for your blessing, Pa."

"Oh, that's easy. You have my blessing. I just thought maybe you wanted me to like it."

Then Pa went out to do the chores.

Two days later, on Sunday afternoon, Bernice got out her stationary box. She was the sister closest in age to Arlene and the one most likely to be chosen as guardian of Arlene's secrets. Bernice carried the greatest potential to be hurt by the Christmas revelation. As her baby Danny struggled to get at her pen and paper, she poured out her heart to Arlene:

> I could hardly get to sleep Friday evening. It will be hard to
> see you leave the states. Oh! So hard. When I think of the long
> time you'd be gone and what can happen while you're away. I
> don't want this letter to make you feel blue, because really you
> need not feel that. You've made the biggest, highest, noblest
> decision any person can ever make. To love and serve him with
> your whole life. I guess the reason why I cry is because it's just
> so grand.

5

You-Will-Be-Good, Daughter-of-John

Mon. M.A.F. arrived unexpectedly to get Eleanor and me. Left Pibor 11 A.M. Nasir at last!! Nuers and Marian at plane. Ann from Gospel Recordings just leaving. Acacia trees in full bloom.

April 25, 1955

Arlene saved her tears for when she was away from family. On the bus, headed to her final semester of nurses training, she sat among strangers, hardly caring what they saw in her reddened eyes. She had broken Pa's heart, but she had received his blessing. She was across the final threshold. There was no turning back.

When she had told Reverend De Jong about her glowing, she knew only that she was called to go away. She did not know where. Now her task was to continue communications with the name on the torn triangle. She waited until January 13, the day she received her graduation pictures. That same day, she sent one of those pictures to the Board of Foreign Missions, along with the personal information form she had completed long before. If the answer came back no, then she was determined not to be dissuaded but to seek opportunity elsewhere.

The response was quick and affirmative, setting in motion the possibility of becoming a missionary of the Reformed Church in America. Physical examinations, a psychological exam, recommendation letters, and interviews followed. Arlene wrote out her personal biography, including a lengthy statement of faith. She asserted, "Jesus Christ is my personal Savior," and admitted, "As a child, I considered prayer merely as a necessary habit. Later it became and has remained a necessary part of my daily life."

In October, Arlene took the train to Coopersville, Michigan, where she was put up overnight with the family of a local veterinarian. As a farm girl and medical professional, Arlene felt right at home that evening when she was asked to assist with a cow having a difficult labor. The next day, a collection of missions candidates sat for a day of interviews, culminating with dinner, speeches, and prayers. Years of Arlene's life huddled at the door to hear her denomination proclaim, "You are God's emissary. With our utmost blessing, go."

Ruth Ransom, the name from the torn triangle, pulled Arlene aside and asked, "Have you ever ridden in a plane?" No, she had not. Miss Ransom told her not to take the train home but to go home another way. Arlene flew to Chicago, safely navigated the transfer to train, and soon found herself seated in the family Pontiac after Pa picked her up at the train station in Le Mars. By now, she had traveled more extensively than anyone in her immediate family—and more than most women in Sioux County. The world was changing, and Arlene had a front-row seat.

An immediate need arose that changed Ransom's plans for a more methodical transition for Arlene. A missionary nurse stationed in southern Sudan had fallen in love and resigned her post to join her soon-to-be-husband elsewhere. Love was one of Miss Ransom's greatest human resource challenges. This time, love left a family physician without a nurse at a riverside clinic serving thousands of the Nuer tribe and hundreds of Arab locals in the difficult-to-access rural heart of the ninth largest country in the world. Ransom hoped to convince the mission board to forgo the usual required year of language and cultural preparation for this nurse's replacement, a replacement she already had in mind. She was now grateful that Arlene was not as young as the typical mission recruit. Arlene's emotional and spiritual maturity, discipline, and work experience prepared her to face the cross-cultural rigors into which she would be suddenly thrown. Like Queen Esther, Arlene seemed to have been chosen "for such a time as this."

The mission board agreed with Ransom. The appointment was announced, and the telephone lines of Sioux Center were set on fire: Arlene Schuiteman was going to Africa!

The village of Nasir, in what was then Anglo-Egyptian Sudan, was the site of a decades-old mission station with brick buildings, glass windows, generator-powered lighting, and even a diesel-powered refrigerator. Arlene would not be living in a grass hut and sleeping on the floor as the locals did, but neither did she need to ship her own furniture at this time. Arlene would share housing with two other single American women. Eleanor Vandevort ("Vandy") was a linguist, translating the Gospel of John into Nuer. *Nuer* (pronounced "new AIR") was the tribal language and also the name of the native people. Writings about this tribal group were few and commonly used the term "Nuer," but the Nuer also referred to themselves as *Naath*, which simply means "the people."

Clusters of grass-roofed Nuer *tukls* dotted the countryside surrounding the government town of Nasir. Nasir held amenities such as a market, post office, police station, clinic, school, and steamship dock. Although the tribal language was Nuer, the town language was Arabic.

Arlene's other future roommate was Marian Farquhar, who had lived in the Sudan for ten years. Marian was a teacher, pioneering education for females since the Arab-controlled government school was for boys only.

Marian's welcome letter arrived at the farm—exuding energy, chattiness, and good humor—helping Arlene's enthusiasm to make her home in northeast Africa. Here's a bit of what Marian wrote:

I'm so eager to meet you in person. There are lots of rocky times ahead for you, but it's really fun to abandon yourself into the Lord's hands like Noah: no tiller, no sail, no compass. "Be careful for nothing; but in everything by prayer and supplication with thanksgiving . . ."

I could tell you what we do with our leisure time. We don't have any. I'm the teacher. Vandy's our Bible translator, a real language expert, and a bit on the incorrigible side. Nuer is our language and our people.

Our house is not as private as it might be, but you can always cry in the shower.

Bring your bathing suit. Vandy wouldn't be caught dead in the river, but the rest of us LIVE in it during the dry season (January through April). In very truth, the usual schedule is: a small dip before lunch, lunch and a nap in the wet bathing suit, another dip to re-wet before the afternoon's stint, and then sometimes another cooling off just at dusk. And that makes the weather very livable!

Bring your rifle or a shotgun; our house needs a shotgun!

I hope I haven't scared you out. I'm oh so glad you're coming. May the Lord bless you very specially as you make last minute preparations and say goodbyes and embark on this GREAT ADVENTURE.

Love, Marian

Marian's breeziness masked her deep understanding that Arlene would need all the bolstering she could receive. A typical mission term was five years. Arlene would not return home during her first term, nor was anyone from Sioux Center likely to visit. She was not dropping off the planet, but her sisters and friends would get married without Arlene's attendance. Nieces and nephews would be born and take their first steps. Funerals would be held, even before Arlene had received word that someone had died.

There was no telephone in Nasir. Arlene was about to go five years without hearing her mother's voice. There would be telegraph and mail service, but the timing of delivery could vary by days or even weeks. Sending packages would always be a lengthy and risky proposition. Arlene was instructed to carry on her person any item from home she wanted to be certain to have in Africa.

Arrival on the African continent would require travel by car, train, ship, and plane—which would get her only as far as Khartoum in northern Sudan. Her ultimate destination would require a truck, a small plane, or a boat, depending on the month of travel. Each year's rainy season made roads impassable, and the dry season lowered the river to a shallow trickle.

Arlene packed a small amount of everyday clothes since she could buy clothes in the Sudan. She packed eleven nurse uniforms, however, that had been hand sewn by a neighbor lady who lived at the farm across the road to the southeast—cap-sleeved, crinkle crepe, and white cotton, since polyester was far too hot for the Sudan. And five pairs of white canvas shoes.

The bulk of luggage space was given over to medical supplies, cooking supplies, and office supplies (especially typing paper and carbon paper since mail would be her connection to the world). Although Arlene was always reading, she allowed no space for books, as they were too heavy. She carried only her Bible, Lettie B. Cowman's collection of devotional writings *Streams in the Desert*, and John Baillie's *A Diary of Private Prayer*—and, of course, her own new *Five-Year Diary*.

Two days before Thanksgiving, her Uncle Ed pulled into the farmyard with his pickup. Uncle Ed and Pa loaded four barrels and a trunk. With great pride, Uncle Ed drove the containers safely to Sioux City, where they would soon be Africa-bound, racing Arlene to see which would arrive first in Nasir.

Arlene's church also swelled with pride and committed to paying her entire annual support. A representative from denominational headquarters in New York City made a special visit to the Sioux Center consistory. Meaning no offense, he asked if Arlene's church would be willing to refrain from paying Arlene's entire support. It would be better, he argued to the men on the church's leadership team, to have other churches across the country involved. His position was reluctantly accepted.

On a mid-December Thursday evening after chores, the church gathered for a commissioning service. The choir sang "Send Me There." Arlene wore her green dress, the same one she planned to wear when she climbed the gangplank onto the ship in the New York Harbor. Reverend De Jong presided that evening, repeating the ancient question from Isaiah 6, "Whom shall I send, and who will go for us?"

This time, Arlene was not sitting upstairs in the gallery. She was standing on the platform. This time, she spoke her response out loud: "Here am I. Send me."

There was a hush in the room. Some recall the sound of crying.

A member of the Board of Foreign Missions of the RCA was present to pronounce the official commission of the denomination. His name was Maurice Te Paske (known in town as "Maurie"), an attorney, longtime mayor of Sioux Center, and a member of Arlene's church. No one was surprised to see Maurie read the commissioning statement, "I commission you to take the Gospel of our Lord Jesus Christ unto all the world."

Maurie was an experienced public speaker, and if there was a quiver in his voice that day, there was good reason. His affinity with the Schuiteman family had been deepened by his own circumstances. Earlier that fall, a tragic auto accident had left his mother

Agnes dead and his wife Vera permanently injured; she was now recuperating ten hours away in a Chicago hospital.

One night during that dreadful season, Maurie was up at two in the morning. He sat at his desk and typed Arlene a note to encourage her through the separation she and her family were about to face. As he typed, his mask of Dutch demeanor slipped aside, if only for a minute:

> *I would not pretend to be able to understand what goes into a decision such as yours—that is something so particularly holy and sacred.*
>
> *But may I just share with you that I had a particularly rough time of it myself this past Sunday evening—Vera is usually in very good spirits when I telephone her [at the hospital] each evening, but on this particular occasion she was so very lonesome that she broke down, and naturally that was rather heart-breaking. . . .*
>
> *I was just wasting some time at my desk . . . trying to pick up a few items, and with the books was the well-worn Bible with "Maurie and Vera" on the cover, and inscribed inside as follows, "Presented with affection to Mr. Maurice Te Paske and Miss Vera Kreykes at their wedding. Psalm 37:5." I turned to that reference and through misty eyes read the verse, "Commit thy way unto the Lord; trust also in Him; and He shall bring it to pass."*
>
> *And how true!—in ourselves we are so very weak at these times of emotional stress. . . .*
>
> *Please share my thoughts with your parents who have every right to be grateful that their home has been the environment in which you made your decision.*
>
> *You are in the thoughts and prayers of hundreds of us, and with continuing appreciation, I remain,*
>
> > *Sincerely,*
> > *Maurice*

Arlene would always remember Maurie's mother Agnes as the Sunday school teacher who first taught her to sing "Jesus Loves Me."

The day after Christmas, the Schuiteman sisters delivered Pa, Ma, and Arlene to the train in Le Mars, Iowa. So began over two months of goodbyes that would have the Schuitemans almost calling out in agony, "Can this parting be over already?!" Arlene sat behind Pa and Ma on the train so they would not see her tears as the train rolled eastward across the gentle rise and fall of the Iowa hills. The plan was for the three of them to stay at Aunt Minn and Uncle Andrew's in Buffalo, New York, and on December 30, Ma and Pa were supposed to be standing on the dock, waving Arlene's ship out of New York Harbor.

Arlene's Sudanese visa was somehow waylaid, however, delaying her departure across the ocean. Pa and Ma could not wait with her indefinitely. So, at 8:10 a.m. on January 3, it was Arlene who stood on the platform waving to Pa and Ma as they climbed aboard the train headed west to the farm.

In late February, Arlene called home to say that the visa had finally arrived. Her departure was set for March 10, but somehow Arlene's sister Joyce got the wrong message. She thought Arlene had called home to say that she was leaving immediately. Joyce thought she'd missed her chance to say a final goodbye and was frantic. Pa and Ma decided it would be best for all concerned if Arlene came home one last time. On March 1, Arlene took the second plane ride of her life, with layovers in Philadelphia, Detroit, and Chicago, arriving in Omaha in the wee hours. She sat in the airport overnight and caught the bus to Sioux City, where her folks picked her up.

Even though Joyce had a terrible flu, she came to the farm to be with Arlene. Extended family and friends were in and out all week. Arlene would need an ocean voyage to catch up on her rest, but the sacrifice was worth the joy of a few more days with her tribe.

On March 8, Pa and Ma's wedding anniversary, they drove Arlene, along with Milly and Grada, to Sioux City, where she caught the flight back to New York. This time, she walked up the gangplank and onto the *Scythia* on schedule. The ship's purser thought she must be someone important because he was holding a huge basket of mail that had arrived for her. Arlene had not really left home— home was following her and always would.

The crossing took ten days. After two lovely days in London visiting the British Museum and catching Shakespeare's *As You Like It* at the Old Vic, Arlene boarded a plane to Rome, Cairo, and, at last, the Sudan. In the capital city of Khartoum, she heard the Muslim call to prayer for the first time and saw the palatial homes of the governmental officials.

Nine days later, she flew south to Malakal. After several days of meeting fellow missionaries, she climbed in the back of an open truck piled high with supplies and other passengers heading east on dirt trails that reminded Arlene of driving the Model A to Plato Township. It was Holy Week, and on Good Friday night, Arlene had her first glimpse of giraffes loping across the flat savanna. The sun slipped beneath the distant horizon, and the rural African night grew darker than Arlene had ever known her Iowa farm to be. Then the Sudanese stars came out, closer and more radiant. Everything was beautiful. When the truck pulled into Nasir in the middle of the night, Arlene discovered that her future housemates were not in town. She was shown to a bed on the porch overlooking the river. As much as she wanted to stay put at Nasir, she was needed for a couple of weeks further south at Pibor. Arlene jolted through Holy Saturday on the back of the truck, arriving in time for supper at the Akobo mission station. After Easter Sunday worship, they continued on to the south, arriving in Pibor at sundown. There she met the incorrigible Vandy, who would become Arlene's dear and lifelong friend.

Finally, finally, on the last Monday of April, the Missionary Aviation Fellowship plane appeared in the piercing blue sky, landed on the burned grass, and piled Arlene and Vandy aboard. Within an hour, they touched down on the runway just outside of Nasir. Marian and a jumble of Nuers paraded the travelers into town. The acacia trees were in their glory, and when a breeze came dancing along the river, a fragrant red carpet floated down over Arlene's yard. Welcome home.

On Wednesday morning, two Nuer men stood at the screened-in veranda clapping their hands sharply, eager to share their good news. When one of the cooks came to the door, Gac Rik spoke to him through the screen: "We wish to speak to the person who has just arrived."

The daily rain had ceased. The wide sky was swept clean for a beautiful day.

Inside the house, Arlene was unpacking the barrels that her Uncle Ed had so carefully delivered to Sioux City and which had been waiting patiently for Arlene's arrival. She was grateful to discover that absolutely nothing had broken in transit.

When the cook tugged at her elbow, she rose quickly, but not quickly enough. Gac Rik and Gac Dwac were calling impatiently: "Come out! We have decided!"

The two men were dressers at the clinic, essentially nurse's aids. They followed the doctors' and nurses' orders, caring for the patients and ensuring a clean environment. For some of the workers, this good employment became a first step toward higher education, perhaps even physician's school in Khartoum and a career as a medical professional.

Arlene was expecting this visit from Gac Rik and Gac Dwac. She knew there had been discussion ever since they met Arlene's plane when it landed on the grassy strip northeast of town. At that time, they had spoken to Arlene in English and showed her around the clinic. The two men were observing her personality as part of the local naming custom. They had considered usual names such as "Daughter of a Cow" and "Tall Palm Tree." She, however, had learned so much Nuer in her first two days that they arrived at what they felt was the perfect name.

Arlene opened the screen door and stepped outside. She spoke their names as she had been taught: "Guy Dwietch" and "Guy Rick." She would learn later that Nuer spelling is nothing like English.

"Hello, Gac Dwac, Gac Rik."

"*Mal mi goaa* [Is it peace]? We have chosen your name. But first you must tell us something."

Arlene laughed. "What must I tell you?"

"We do not know your father's name."

They were asking for Arlene's family name or surname, but Arlene did not immediately understand. So instead, she simply said, "My father's name is John."

"Then that is easy. We will call you 'Nya BiGoaa Jon.'"

Arlene repeated the name to be sure she had the pronunciation correct. "Nya BiGoaa" uses all soft vowels sounds, and the accent is on the second syllable: *nyah-BIH-gwah*.

The men grinned to hear the new name coming from her mouth. "Do you want to know what it means?"

"It means something?" Arlene asked with a twinkle in her eye.

"All Nuer names mean something! 'Nya' means you are not married. All females are 'Nya' until they are married."

"When they are married, they change their names?"

"No. They wait until they have children. Then, when they are ready, they take the name of the firstborn child. Like 'Mother of whatever the child's name is.' But they do that after the child begins to speak and starts using that name."

"The child changes its mother's name?"

The two men looked at each other. How could they make her understand? "What do you call your mother?"

"Her name is Johanna."

"Is that what you call her?"

"No. We call her Ma."

"What does that mean?"

"Mother."

"Yes! You understand! You have changed your mother's name from her childhood name. We do the same in Nuerland!"

Arlene smiled. She somewhat understood the men's point, although she didn't like the idea that in the process her mother had lost her name. The two Guys continued.

"What do you call an unmarried woman?"

"In America, we say Miss."

"You say 'Miss' and we say *Nya*."

"In Nuer, you say *Nya*?"

"*Awhn* [Yes]! And BiGoaa means, 'You will be good.' So your whole name means, 'Miss You-Will-Be-Good, Daughter-of-John!'"

"I will be good?"

"Yes! You will be good, because you have learned so much Nuer in only two days."

"*Ci locda teth* [Thank you for my name]."

The men grinned and said her name again, very proud of themselves: "Nya BiGoaa Jon!"

Later, when Arlene told her fellow missionaries her Nuer name, they said, "Oh? When is that? When will you be good?" Her new name immediately became both a compliment and a tool for teasing. Therefore, it stuck.

6

Fishing Day

*Fri. Marian and I left here at 9:30 to go to fishing
of pool 4 miles across river. Resulted in fight
between various villages 'cause some went in water
too early. Chiefs imprisoned. Home at 3 P.M.*

May 27, 1955

"Nya BiGoaa! Nya BiGoaa Jon! It's today!"

The news flew through the clinic, the school, and all of Nasir. The three chiefs of the nearby villages had decided. Today, Friday, this morning, right now would be the annual community Fishing Day at a particular large pool four miles from Nasir, on the far side of the Sobat River. Even though the heavy rains of the season had not started falling, the Sobat had been steadily on the rise because of the spring rains in the mountains of Ethiopia to the east. The river was seeping over its banks, re-forming the swamps, and raising the levels of the low-lying pools. In particular, the best and largest fishing pool would not yet be too deep for wading, and it would be restocked with Nile perch. Now was the perfect time to walk in and spear a fish. Although one could fish with a net, today skill with the spear would be on display. Today's haul would be dried and stored, providing hundreds of families with a full larder at this very hungry time of the year.

Strict rules governed this sudden and festive opening day. Everyone was to have a fisherman's chance. Fishing early was a crime. The plan this morning was to stand at the water's edge, spear in hand, and wait for the chiefs to give the signal.

Classes and clinics were immediately cancelled. There would be little use trying to keep any Nuer in town on Fishing Day. They would all be heading out to either fish or cheer on those who were fishing. Marian would have been content to claim the day as a vacation—like a snow day back in Iowa—but Arlene had heard about Fishing Day, and she was agitating to go see what the fuss was about. Truth be told, Marian had not yet witnessed the annual Fishing Day, even though she had lived here for a decade. So, when Arlene said she would love to go, Marian required minimal persuasion. The news that the nurse and the teacher would be attending Fishing Day spread nearly as fast as the news of Fishing Day itself.

There was some leftover creamed chicken in the icebox. Since the women didn't know how long the trip would take, they made two sandwiches apiece for a quickly packed lunch. They drank some milk and filled their canteens with water. Arlene changed out of her clinic uniform into her blue jeans and long-sleeved checkered shirt, plopped her wide-brimmed hat on her head, pulled on her high-top boots, and slung her rifle over her shoulder. Marian grabbed her gun as well, since neither of them wanted to encounter a cobra or python without some defense at hand. Arlene looped her camera around her neck, and they were off.

Two of the household staff, Gac and Gat Luak, were delighted to be their guides. They took Marian's boat across the Sobat, alongside dozens of dugout canoes ferrying hundreds of men, women, and children. The normally smooth water splashed with excitement. The parade of small watercrafts circumnavigated a bamboo grove that had become an island now that the river had risen. They continued paddling into the swamp until the grass was simply too thick and it was time to wade toward higher ground.

As the foursome climbed out of the boat, Gac suddenly said, "Uh-oh." He was looking toward Nor, the village down by Picnic Island.

"What's wrong?" asked Marian in Nuer.

"Those people. They're going the wrong way."

"Why?"

"They're just going now to get the chief of the Cieng Thiep village. That means it'll be one o'clock before the signal is given to go in the water."

Marian smiled at Arlene and muttered, "Africa moves in creeper gear."

Gac quickly adjusted the plan. "You keep walking. We're going to wait for some of our people. We'll catch up to you."

"Which way?" Marian asked. Gac raised his chin toward the far horizon. No further direction was needed since they could just migrate with the crowds. So, off they went over ground that was mostly dry but had turned spongy in places. At first, Arlene attempted to avoid the wet spots. She soon realized it was no use as her feet became caked with mud and the bottoms of her trouser legs were soaked.

As they walked, they were joined by clusters of men, women, and children, who chattered at Marian and Arlene. Arlene caught nary a word, but her smiles and nods were returned. After a few minutes, each group would move on ahead. The Nuer were generally taller than the two women and more fleet of foot. These locals moved with confidence, eager to claim an excellent spot by the water's edge.

The small clusters became larger clusters, and soon there was a solid stream of moving bodies. The young men carried two or more tall spears. Beyond that accessory, one might call them naked, but there is no such word as *naked* in Nuer. The Nuer would say that a person was "empty" or "full," referring to whether that person was wearing jewelry. On this day of days, the fisherman wore his jewelry. He had his spears and decorations—he was full.

Not only were the young men full, but the air was full. The men were singing. The singing was not in itself unusual. Someone was always singing in Nuerland. Songs could be heard throughout the entire morning's walk to the pool. Individuals sang at full voice without inhibition. Singing was not considered a special skill. Singing was life. To breathe was to sing. Everyone sang. But today was different. Special songs proclaimed group identity and pride. Music fueled group intent, challenge, and even warning.

Shortly before noon, the women came upon a large group resting on the grass. There was no pool in sight.

"Let's continue on and rest when we get to the pool," said Marian. They continued walking. After a while, they arrived at a place they thought must be near the pool since a crowd was gathered, so they sat down. Everyone came over for a visit.

"*Mal e mi goaa* [Is it peace with you]?"

"*Awhn, mal e* [Yes, it is]."

Even Arlene knew this little greeting, but if she gave it, she would soon be asked follow-up questions. She would have to shake her head and point to Marian, who was having her own troubles keeping up—not because of her skill with the language, but because of the number of greeters and questioners.

Sitting there, Arlene wondered how many people were within view. By counting a group of fifty, she was able to scan for similar-sized clusters. She counted twenty clusters, which meant a thousand people were already nearby.

A schoolboy said to Marian, "Why don't you follow me around over there for a better view?" Immediately a committee formed to consider the best viewing spot and the best way to walk there. Finally, a decision was made, and they followed their Nuer hosts. Marian reported to Arlene, "Turns out, this is not the fishing pool. We have a ways to go."

Before long, Gat Luak came rushing up to reclaim his role as guide. "I don't think anyone will get angry if I take you right up to the water."

In an effort to make conversation, Marian said, "Arlene counted a thousand people here."

"These are only the Cieng Man Yual," said Gat Luak. He meant that these were all from the Nasir side of the river.

"Where are the other two villages, the Cieng Thiep and Cieng Wang?"

"Oh, you'll see them."

Once again, they followed Gat Luak. Soon the grass sloped and a large fishing pool spread out before them. Then they heard it: the song of the Cieng Thiep. The song was sometimes call and response, and sometimes in unison—and sometimes the singing was nearly overwhelmed by the caws, howls, and ululations. The song and sounds seemed perfectly planned and cued but also completely spontaneous, with an energetic ebb and flow that seemed organic. The effect was both wild and relaxed. The sound punched, fell away, and rose again.

Then the source of all this sound appeared—a solid black body. If the Cieng Man Yual were a thousand, then the Cieng Thiep were two thousand.

As if in answer, from the other side of the pool, there came line after line of tall fishing spears walking and dancing through the high grass. Then there was another sound, with its own eccentricity—the song of the Cieng Wang! Marian said later that this meeting of the three Ciengs was one of the most thrilling events she had ever witnessed.

An old man who would not be going into the water, a man from the Cieng Thiep village by Picnic Island, came to speak with Marian. When she used a Nuer pronoun that included Arlene and herself among the Cieng Man Yual people, the old man laughed. These white women might live on the Nasir side of the river, but did they really consider themselves Cieng Man Yual? He laughed and laughed.

Directly in front of Marian and Arlene, a group of Cieng Man Yual boys waded through the swamp to the very edge of the pool. Arlene raised her camera.

Suddenly the old man of the Cieng Thiep threw his head back and sniffed the wind like an old warhorse. He grabbed Gat Luak by the arm. "Why are the people *cicking the cick* [singing a war cry]?"

"Oh, it's nothing . . . they're playing," Gat Luak answered casually, but he had a very serious look on his face. In a moment, they all knew that Gat Luak was expressing a wishful thought as the sound grew louder and louder. Turning toward the sound, they saw hordes of the Cieng Thiep sweeping down upon them.

"Get out! Get out!" screamed Gat Luak. The Cieng Thiep clearly thought that the people from the other side of Nasir had begun to fish before the signal had been given. The Cieng Man Yual splashed back out of the swamp, but they began *cicking the cick* themselves. The sound was deafening, but no one was letting up. Now the Cieng Wang were *cicking the cick* as well and running from the far side of the pool. Thousands of angry young men were heading to where they imagined there might be action. Although they were not coming straight toward Marian and Arlene, the two had a front-row seat.

The songs grew into a great chant, four thousand voices strong. "It's a *Kor*! It's a *Kor*! [It's a battle]!"

The sound of the chant carried back to the women preparing for the expected fish supper in the cattle camps by the edge of the Sobat. The thump of the chant echoed on across the river to Nasir where Dr. Gordon sat in the clinic. He grabbed his binoculars and climbed as quickly as he could up the rungs to the top of the windmill. The horrendous sound carried on into the center of Nasir where the Arab police chief called his men to their horses. Soon the sound of galloping joined the war cry. Then there was the sound of horses splashing through the water, swimming toward the commotion coming from the far side of the swamps.

Back at the pool, the chanters were no longer coming directly at one another. They milled and circled, pounding the earth with their war dance. No one looked afraid to fight. No one was losing face. There was no backing down. Some men rushed over to their women and children, who had come along to help carry the fish home. Those men sent their families away and then returned to the huge huddles, spears in hand.

Gat Luak tried to spread himself wide in front of Marian and Arlene.

"Any fishing today?" Marian asked him.

"No fishing today."

Two little girls, covering their ears, came and stood by the white women. The littlest one, trembling all over, grabbed a hold of Arlene's leg and would not let go.

Bit by bit, almost imperceptibly, the clusters of chanting, singing, dancing men began orbiting away from one another. They were caught in a dilemma. They dared not be accused of starting the battle, and they dared not be taunted for turning away. The three Ciengs, who at first had come so thrillingly together for this annual fishing event, were now engaged in the subtle ritual of guarding their honor while at the same time avoiding war.

After twenty minutes or so—one could hardly think of time—Marian asked Gat Luak if he thought it was safe for them to start for home.

"*Awhn.*"

They turned and started across the no-man's land between the villages. The old man shouted after them, "Look at what you Cieng Man Yual did!" Although he was merely teasing, he was not laughing. The littlest girl still clung to Arlene's leg, while her sister kept glancing back at the mass of men. After about a half an hour, Arlene also looked. The Cieng Thiep had faded away toward their *tukls* down by the island, and the Cieng Wang had disappeared into the tall grass opposite the pool.

Crowds of the Cieng Man Yual kept passing the slow-moving group on their way toward the river. Some of the young men were still *cicking the cick*, perhaps because they did not want to admit that they were the ones who had caused it all. Just as Marian and Arlene wondered where they should take the girls, their mother came frantically looking for them. "We were fine!" the girls insisted as their mother dragged them away, chattering with that angry parental voice that meant she was so relieved.

Marian and Arlene finally reached the river at three o'clock. Gat Luak had turned back to see if he could be a force for calm. He told them later that the mounted police had rounded up the three chiefs and taken them off to jail for a few days to see what had caused the ruckus and to deter future disturbances of the peace.

The next day, there was surprising talk all over town about how the white women ran and ran. This gossip was patently false, but the rumor could hardly be unspread. In addition, many people asked Marian and Arlene, "Why didn't you shoot your guns?" Arlene wondered why such a question would be asked. Were they suggesting that she was in more danger than she thought? Did they believe that the town nurse would have fired her gun with the intention of killing another person? Arlene was baptized into Christ, and Christ lived in her. Christ told her to love her enemies, not to raise her rifle and shoot them. She had been raised with guns in the house, and she believed in the gift of technology. She wielded the scalpel, after all; but she had been schooled in the medical ethics of *Primum non nocere* (First, do no harm) and Jesus' teaching that she should turn the other cheek.

Arlene did not yet understand the deep-seated belief among the Nuer that those with guns have the power—a belief that would lead to much pain if the Ciengs ever got their hands on automatic weapons. The Nuer worldview was to put one's trust in the chief and in the spear. Arlene's worldview was:

Do not put your trust in princes,
    in mortals, in whom there is no help.
When their breath departs, they return to the earth;
    on that very day their plans perish.
Happy are those whose help is the God of Jacob,
    whose hope is in the Lord their God,
who made heaven and earth.
        Psalm 146:3–6a (NRSV)

Five days after the incident at the fishing pool, news swept through town that it was once again Fishing Day. The police attended this time, but Arlene stayed in Nasir to answer her mail, as a lorry had arrived with forty letters from home. It would be the last truck of the season, because the hard rains had started to fall.

Maybe next year Arlene would be ready to visit another Fishing Day. First, she would need to investigate whether she and Marian had played an unwitting role in almost starting a war.

7

South Sudan, July 1955

1. Praise God—Ten days alone and enjoyed it.
2. Trust God for Kuoth Brothers.
3. Five formula babies—God saved
   them all—even premies.
4. Dr. Gordon's, Vi's, and my language.
5. Arlys Ann's birth.

Arlene's prayer summary
(end of July 1955)

July brought the heart of the rainy season. Annual precipitation at Nasir was about a third more than Sioux Center's annual precipitation. In Nasir, half the year was dry, and then the rain fell, more and more. This much rain in an Iowa growing season would ruin everything—the fields, the gardens, the landscaping. Here in southern Sudan, the water drained into the river or swamps, and individual households simply moved or built dikes and trenches to control the water. Farming was accomplished on foot, since wheels could hardly negotiate the mud.

Back in Iowa, the corn was already knee-high. On the Schuiteman farm, they were bailing hay, cutting oats, and canning beans. The lazy summer evenings were filled with baseball games, drive-in movies, and hot dog roasts. On quiet nights, you could hear the corn grow.

Arlene loved her old home, but she was also growing to love her new home. When would the sheen of African newness wear away? Arlene's diary suggests that it never would.

Friday, July 1
"Walked out to take pictures of planting."

Vandy decided it was time to take this Iowa farm girl to see Nuer farming. The arrival of the rainy season had softened the ground. Planting of crops was mostly complete, and now farmers would be fussing over the early growth. Carrying their cameras, Nya BiGoaa (Arlene) and Nyarial (Vandy) slogged through the mud, heading away from the river, across the swamps, and into the open country.

Arlene never heard the story of Vandy receiving her Nuer name, but she knew Vandy had a name of honor. The name "Nyarial" meant "daughter of the black and white cow." Cows are the life-blood of Nuerland. In Vandy's home state of Pennsylvania, naming a woman after a beast, especially a milk cow, would have been beyond strange. Imagine calling your daughter "Guernsey" or "Holstein." In Nuerland, however, Vandy had been given one of the most respectable names.

Arlene felt at home in the open countryside. The scattered *tukls* and cow barns of Nuer farmland stood in her mind's eye next to the farmsteads strewn across Iowa. There were, of course, significant differences. Nuer property had no fences or roads, but all the locals seemed to know well enough where one property ended and another began. Rather than blue jeans, the farmers in the Sudan wore their birthday suits, squatted on their haunches, and with one hand manipulated a pointed stick that accomplished all the tasks that, back home, required plow, disk, planter, and tractor.

Each Sudanese farmer planted purplish dura seed that yielded a sorghum grain to be pounded into powder and cooked into a nourishing porridge. These farmers of Eden were following a rhythm they believed to be as old as the earth. They had sun, rain, soil, river, cattle, language, love, family, tribe, and freedom. They had neither pockets nor money, but these richest men in the world were pleased that two white women had come to admire their work.

Saturday, July 2
"Thrilling experience. Clouds and moonlight."

A telegram arrived, urging Marian to leave immediately. She had been expected in Malakal for a missions committee meeting, and a complex transportation solution had presented itself. If she could get to Akobo in the south, there was a grass airstrip that had not yet been dissolved to mud by the rain. One of the last Missionary Aviation Fellowship flights of the season was headed to Malakal and had room for Marian if she could get there in time. Malakal was two hundred miles northwest of Nasir, but Marian would need to motorboat eastward to where the Pibor joined the Sobat, continuing south along the Ethiopian border toward Akobo. Another boat would rendezvous with her somewhere on the Pibor and then ferry her south. If the plan worked, she would catch the plane and be in Malakal the next day. Otherwise, she would have to wait for a steamboat on the Sobat, and no one knew when the next steamer would arrive.

Marian needed Vandy to go along to pilot the motorboat back to Nasir, and Vandy asked Arlene to come along so she would not be traveling home alone that evening.

It was late in the day when the small crew waved down the other small boat coming up the Pibor. Saying goodbye, Marian stepped from one hull to the other. Arlene and Vandy turned their boat back to the north, but they had not yet reached the Sobat junction when the African night fell. They continued upriver by the light of the moon, staying as best as they could in the deep water of the river's center, peering for logs or snags. The river perch rose to the surface to feed on early evening insects, and the silvery fish bodies slipping up and down in the moonlit water gave the normally placid surface of the Sobat a muscular feel, inspiring a mixture of dread and delight.

Arlene had been raised on a farm miles and miles from the nearest river. She never learned to swim. Her whole neighborhood of farm families remembered the deep grief of the Wesselink family when their little girl had wandered across the yard and somehow climbed into the cattle tank and drowned. Seeking to avoid their own tragedy, some families would make sure everyone took swimming lessons. Other families, like Arlene's, chose not to take chances. On the few occasions their family took a day trip to a state park with a river, Ma would always say, "No one go near the water!"

On this African night, Arlene and Vandy traveled without life jackets, even though the river had risen with the rain and was thirty feet deep in places. If they did capsize, staying afloat would be the least of their worries, since it was now crocodile season. Arlene wondered how she could write to her family about this journey without causing Ma's heart to leap into her throat.

Due to the noise of the motor, they did not speak but kept their faces to the wind and their eyes on the water. They took turns at the helm, another new adventure for Arlene in a whole year of novelties. She thought, "I am definitely here in Africa!" If she were ever tempted to be anxious, she was sustained by the sheer wonder of it all.

A cloud blew in, lightly covering the moon. That luminescent mist towered over the river like a pillar of fire, leading Nyarial and Nya BiGoaa rejoicing into harbor at Nasir.

Sunday, July 3
"Kong free at court."

The intrepid boaters rose at dawn for a prayer meeting. Later in the morning, someone took a metal rod and struck the flat piece of iron suspended by wire from a tree, calling the small band of Christians to come to the worship *tukl*. Vandy was the preacher of the day, and her text was the story of Stephen the martyr. That afternoon, news came as part of the ongoing story of the acts of the church—the court had released Kong Jing! The local Christians knew Kong Jing to be a singer of Bible stories. Vandy, an expert in the Nuer language and singer in her own right, would remember and sing Kong Jing's songs for years to come. Why had Kong been imprisoned? The answer was unclear, but the people in Arlene's circle believed that the motivations were both political and religious.

Britain was done with the Sudan, and conversations concerning independent governance could get highly charged. The debate was how to best negotiate the wide ethnic and religious gulf between the Arab/Muslim north and the multi-tribal/polytheist and Christian south. Would Sudan be ruled as one country or two? Would the government be an Islamic state or a federal system? Various attempts were being made to assert power rather than wait for a peaceful transition.

Arlene recorded hints of these tensions in her journal, with cryptic sentences such as "Kong free at court." For the most part, Arlene avoided a written record of her thoughts on these matters. Her letters back to the farm hardly mentioned local politics. She was silent for a couple of reasons. First, she was told by experienced missionary leaders that her letters could be opened and scrutinized and that she should take care not to endanger any of the local Sudanese leaders. Second, she did not want to overly concern her family.

Arlene faced the challenge of how to reassure her family, encourage authentic prayers, and avoid undue negative attention. Following the advice of her missionary colleagues, she told her family that anything they heard on the news was far away from Nasir. Concerning governmental tensions, she tended to write, "We are and always have been just fine." She was not telling the whole truth, but it was the best she could do—and compared to how bad things would be one day, she was right.

Monday, July 4
"Washed hair."

Washing one's hair in the Sudan required the same thing as pretty much everywhere else on the planet: water. In 1955, Nasir had a few options for sources of water, and each option came with effort and risk.

The first option for water was the sink faucet in the mission house. The sink faucet was fed by a well that was pumped by the windmill when there was wind or when the windmill wasn't broken. Well water was the cleanest water available and therefore not used for washing hair.

The second option for water was the shower. A barrel on a platform fed the shower, as well as the toilet tank. The height of the platform provided good water pressure, but the barrel contained water only when it rained or when someone filled it with water they carried from the river. The shower water was not purified and therefore had to be used with care. When the shower and toilet water ran dry, everyone had to wait until the barrel was refilled.

The third option was large pottery jars. These jars were filled with rainwater or water carted from the middle of the river, which was the cleanest. The pottery was designed to permit water to seep through and thereby strain the water. After straining, the water was boiled for drinking or preparing meals. Due to the amount of work involved, jar water was never for washing hair.

The best option for hair-washing water flowed past the front veranda just steps away—the Sobat River. In the dry season, the river ran slowly and was at its muddiest. In the rainy season, which was now, the river ran quickly and was fairly sediment free. The deep river season, however, brought crocodiles. Naturally, Arlene stayed close to shore and didn't close her eyes very long!

To wash her hair, Arlene would wade out to where the boat was moored, rest her bottle of soap in the boat, and dip her head into the river. She did this on Saturday afternoons as part of her preparation for Sunday services, and because the river water had warmed a bit in the heat of the day.

This particular weekend, Arlene had missed her usual Saturday hair washing routine due to the motorboat trip—and, of course, she would not do such a thing as wash her hair on the Lord's Day.

Arlene knew she had a full schedule of clinic duties for Monday morning, so she snuck a bit of faucet water and washed her hair quickly in the sink before breakfast. It made her feel a bit guilty, which earned the event an entry in her journal.

The day turned out to be even busier than she expected. That evening, an excited man came running down the path. Nyakong had delivered a premature baby at three and a half pounds, requiring the services of the local doctor and his nurse. This American Independence Day event would start Arlene on a detective journey that would take the remainder of the month for her to solve.

Tuesday, July 5
"Wish it'd rain."

There was no rain, so the patients kept coming. Usually at this time of year, rain fell in buckets for at least a couple of hours, driving everyone indoors.

Arlene hoped for a downpour so she could get some extra letter writing done before the chug of the next river steamer was heard coming up the river. There were several boats, known by their names *Tamai*, *Nuer*, and *Nakehlia*, and it was past time for one of them to arrive.

Mail came and went sporadically at Nasir, creating a buildup of letters to be answered. Arlene typed her letters on onionskin paper, making carbon copies of up to four at a time. This method allowed her to respond to several family members and friends at once. Her letters were substantial, usually two pages in length. Allowing time for proofreading, each letter would take an hour or more, and she needed to average nearly two letters a day. Without the rain breaks, she would have to write deep into the night, or at least until the kerosene lantern ran dry (the generator was not currently working and there was no electric light).

It would have been a blessing to have at least a *luth ruun* (a heavy rain). If Arlene awoke to the sound of rain, then the clinic would have no patients, school bells would not ring, the cooks would not arrive to make breakfast—the morning would be free.

On occasion, rain would fall for three days straight. Time would slow. Sabbath. A heaven-sent time of rest, which is what Arlene was longing for when she wrote her journal entry late that Tuesday night.

Wednesday, July 6
"Cold. 75°"

Rain! The steady downpour made any temperatures under 80° downright chilly, especially for those Nuer who wore no clothes. Arlene knew precisely what the temperature was because she had brought her little TEL-TRU Room Thermometer and placed it on her dresser. She had purchased the thermometer in Buffalo, New York, when she went on the train to visit her Aunt Minn and Uncle Andrew. That had been Arlene's first trip ever off the farm. Aunt Minn knew how excellent Arlene was at wallpapering, so she offered her nieces Arlene and Harriet a trip to New York City in return for some decorating help. About a decade had passed since that trip, and the little thermometer was holding up just fine.

The *Tamai* dropped off mail and supplies as it headed upriver. In one or two days, the lumbering steamship would turn around and head downriver, pausing at Nasir overnight.

"I'll have to get the wiggle on," Arlene would say, keeping her typewriter hot throughout much of that cold and rainy day.

Thursday, July 7
"Wedding dance."

Nya Ruac Gac held her wedding dance, and Arlene snapped some photos from the roof of the house.

A Nuer wedding dance is the second of two major dances honoring the purchase of a wife. In 1955, a Nuer woman was property, and if she were to marry, she must be bought from her family, with her uncle serving as chief negotiator. The usual price was twenty cows, but the precise number and which specific ones was a matter of lengthy conversation. As negotiations reached their climax, an engagement dance might be held to encourage an agreement. Once the price had been settled and the engagement dance concluded, the consummation of the marriage could take place, along with the gradual payment of the agreed-upon cows. Once the cows were all delivered, they held the wedding dance and the wife moved to her husband's compound. He would build her a house, which he would visit before returning to the barn, where he always slept to protect the cows.

If he could obtain enough cows, he might purchase a second wife—or a third. There was no danger of a wife leaving her husband. The cows bound a wife in service to her husband; for if she ever left him, the cows he had paid for her must be returned, every last one. Moreover, the children from a broken marriage would always remain the property of the husband.

For marriage dances, men painted their faces with colorful makeup made from cow dung and ashes. They wore ivory on their arms, big thick bracelets, and strings of beads around their foreheads, necks, waists, and ankles. Beads could be purchased in the *suk* (market), and all Nuer, from little girls to old men, loved to string colored beads into carefully designed jewelry. Men wore much more jewelry than women did, and any interesting item— such as a safety pin or a piece of bone—could be found dangling from the holes they made in their ears.

Since Arlene's office had a glass window, she would sometimes be surprised to look up and see a man using the window as a mirror to do his final preening on the way to a dance. Small culture shocks, like a strange man fixing his makeup at your window, were an ongoing challenge for Arlene, especially since she had arrived in Nuerland with little orientation. She was receiving both language and cultural training while already on the field. These circumstances were made manageable, however, by the maturity and friendship of

Marian and Vandy. But Marian was gone to Malakal, and tomorrow Vandy would also have to pack up and go.

Friday, July 8
"Vandy slept on Tamai."

The *Tamai* arrived in the afternoon. The *Tamai* and her fellow boats were now the region's only lifelines to the outside world. There would be no trucks or planes until late fall.

Vandy had been temporarily reassigned to help with translating and orientation at the mission station at Ler. Vandy had prepared materials so Arlene's language tutors could keep her progressing. A danger for Arlene was that she would become so caught up in clinic duties she would neglect learning Nuer.

The *Tamai* would pull out at four o'clock Saturday morning and then take several days to travel to Malakal and then on to Ler. Vandy took all her own provisions—cot, mosquito netting, stove, and food. Arlene used the motorboat to transport Vandy's suitcase, books, and travel provisions to the steam vessel. Because of the early morning departure, the two women said goodbye that night. Vandy would wake up somewhere downriver.

As Arlene wrote her journal for the day, she was alone in the house. Lying on her bed on the riverside veranda, she could hear silver-tailed mongooses scampering under the large acacia trees. The recent rains had knocked most of the blossoms out of the trees, making a deep carpet along the riverbank. Where the blossoms had been, starlight poked through, turning the acacias into what looked to Arlene like a row of Christmas trees, sparkling with light.

Saturday, July 9
"Premie doesn't eat well."

Arlene was not yet assigned to regular clinic duties, but she could see that babies were dying. Even though her primary task at present was to acquire language and culture, she assigned herself the

challenge of lowering the infant mortality rate at Nasir. She identified two especially at-risk groups: premature babies and babies who
had no mother to nurse them (the mothers had died in childbirth
or were too anemic to provide nutritious breast milk). To clearly assess the nature of the problem, Arlene decided she would ask family
members to bring the at-risk babies to her house every Saturday,
when she would do weekly comparative weight analyses to see if
each child was growing. One of the dressers would help her interact
with the family member who brought each infant, and Arlene would
put her medical detective skills to work, listening for possible problems. Powdered formula could be distributed during these visits.

Arlene's discovery today was that the premie born earlier this
week was not growing. She had been giving the family powdered
formula, but it was not working. Why? She asked the family to
switch the child from powdered formula to cow's milk. To ensure
bacterial control, she decided to provide milk from her own refrigerator, as her household's supply of milk had been properly pasteurized. She fed the milk to the baby and then asked to see the tiny
child sooner than the following Saturday.

Sunday, July 10
"Gac wants to borrow 1LE."

Marian and Vandy were gone, and the time had come to
test whether Arlene would stick to the house rules having to do
with money.

Since there were no local banks, the funds for the upkeep of
the mission were kept in a locked steel box. This money was used
to purchase food and supplies and to pay the workers. It was the
matter of workers' pay that was about to be tested.

A system had been put in place to guard a worker's cash. The
workers actually preferred not to be paid, but instead to have their
cash stored out of their grasp. If they had cash on them, then relatives and friends felt free to ask for their money, and it was crucial

that they be able to honestly answer, "I have no money." This must mean that they had no money on them and that they had no access to the money. If they had access to the money, it was not really theirs but their family's or the tribe's. Such was the nature of the concept of possession. The money was theirs, but it wasn't. And if they didn't have access to it, then they didn't have it. The system removed access, which, ironically, made the money theirs. Money, to a young Nuer man, was important for one particular purpose: to buy cows. Food could be acquired in many ways, but the best way to acquire cows was with money.

The Nuer employees at the mission were happy with the money saving system. They could procure their money, but never on a whim. The money was available only on certain days, and even then only with advance notice.

The way the system worked was that Arlene would keep track of a worker's hours, and each week she would open the locked steel box. She would transfer the appropriate amount of money to a tin can belonging to each worker. Then she would relock the box. The money stayed out of each worker's reach until a certain day of the month. On the procurement day, and on that day only, a worker could request access to his savings.

Although Sunday was not a day for opening the box, one of the employees, Gac, needed to buy cows to trade for a wife. He asked Nya BiGoaa for access to his funds and if he could borrow one Egyptian Pound (one L.E.) against his future pay.

Arlene had agreed to be house treasurer, and Marian had been overjoyed since Arlene was a superb organizer—but she also had a tender heart. She would need to develop a cold heart to withstand the many polite requests typical of life among the Nuer. If Arlene gave an inch, there would be no keeping the secret, and everyone would want Arlene to be their friend—meaning they would want her to loan them money or buy them a cow. She gulped and said no, but she noted the interchange in her journal in case she needed to remember this day.

Monday, July 11
"Bob shot bustard."

There was a reason to have a gun in Africa. Unless you were good with a spear, you needed a gun for protection and for food. You needed protection primarily from cobras, but you might also cross paths with a crocodile, hippo, hyena, or lion—a panther had once been seen in the mission garden. The Sobat provided fish to eat, but occasionally the palette longed for something more. One could sometimes get a shot at the deer-like waterbuck, a wild goose, or the large, low-flying bustard. The bustard averages four feet from head to tail, standing three feet high on spindly legs. Wingspan can easily stretch to seven feet, and some of the males weigh forty pounds. Although a bustard would provide excellent food for a hungry Nuer family, superstitions related to mythology surrounding the birth of twins kept the Nuer from eating any of the birds or their eggs.

Vandy shot a bustard one Christmas Eve. She came waltzing home and chopped it open—only to discover it was filled with tapeworm. They had canned ham for Christmas dinner instead.

On this July night, Bob Gordon, the mission's primary physician and Arlene's boss, bagged a healthy bustard that cooked up nicely. Bob invited the clinic nurse to join the Gordon family for supper, and Arlene made note of the event in her journal.

During the meal at the Gordons', a runner from the post office came clapping at the door with a telegram. Vandy had sent word that she had docked safely in Malakal.

Tuesday, July 12
"Showed Gatleak some pictures of home."

Each Tuesday started early with a two-hour gathering for disciplined and specific prayer. Arlene attended three or four such gatherings during the week, in addition to her daily private times of prayer. The remainder of her Tuesday mornings were spent on language lessons with Gatleak, one of the teachers from the government boys' school. He was interested in hearing about farming in Iowa, so Arlene took the time to show him pictures of her home, the cattle, the red barns, and snow.

Arlene treated Gatleak's little girl once. She had a sore on her neck, to which Arlene applied ointment, covering it with a dressing. Flies got into the dressing and laid eggs there. When the girl returned to the clinic, Arlene removed the dressing to discover maggots crawling in and around the girl's sore. Arlene called out, "Dr. Gordon! Come!" Bob looked at the situation and calmly said, "That's okay. Those things'll clean the wound." Arlene had read of such a thing, but here was the difference between reading and seeing. She trusted her doctor and simply covered the wound—much to Gatleak's disgust.

Wednesday, July 13
"Lul and marriage talk!!"

Lul Kuoth was one of the men of the church. He was also the head of the mission garden and supervised other workers in the picking and selling of fruits and vegetables. He was married to one wife and had a daughter who attended primary school under Marian's tutelage. Whereas the government provided school only for boys, the mission, through Marian's gifted leadership, was working to provide girls with education and a voice in the culture of the Nuer. Marian was traveling throughout the villages and rural compounds to establish one-room schoolhouses, hiring local teachers and recruiting students.

Lul wanted to procure a second wife, but he was interested in what the Bible had to say on the matter. He had already conversed with Marian, and now he spoke with Arlene.

Arlene knew the standard answer. The apostle Paul wrote letters stating that leaders in the church were to be husbands of one wife. This standard, in the culture of Arlene's upbringing, was generalized to all Christians. In the generalized application of the "husband of one wife" principle (1 Timothy 3:2; Titus 1:6), polygamy was not allowed and church leaders were to be men. Arlene's traditional values were now being tested in this little riverside village. Back home in Sioux Center, women were not yet allowed to serve the church as preachers. Here in Nasir, however, Vandy often preached at Sunday worship. Why shouldn't a woman preach, wondered Arlene? Vandy was an excellent biblical expositor, with a firm grasp of the Bible's original languages as well as the Nuer language of her congregation. Who better? But according to one interpretation of the verse, Vandy would be disqualified from leadership because she could never be "the husband of one wife." And if Arlene wasn't willing to apply a literal reading of the verse in Vandy's case, then what grounds did she have to apply a literal reading to Lul, who wished to have more than one wife?

Arlene knew what Marian would say. Lul's taking of a second wife was not only a violation of the apostle Paul's clear embrace of monogamy, but it was also an expression of the patriarchal system that subjugated women. Jesus had died to set individuals and whole cultures free, and Marian had come to Africa for such a time as this. Teaching Christian monogamy was one of her primary weapons against the evil being done to women, especially as they had so little voice. Yes, Arlene knew what Marian would say. "How can Lul and his kind call themselves Christians!"

Vandy, on the other hand, might remind Arlene of the Old Testament heroes who took more than one wife: Abraham, Jacob, David, Solomon. Vandy might embrace an expositor's nuance, arguing that the apostle Paul did not write that Christians in general were limited to only one wife but specifically church elders. Vandy would remind Arlene of the anthropological view. These Nuer men must have a reason for taking a second wife. Vandy might say that cultural outsiders should be slow to judge.

Arlene was a good listener. She stuck to the basics of the gospel: Jesus was good news for sinners of every kind, of which she was one. Arlene gave Lul some things to think about, but she did not provide him a definitive answer. She saved the exclamation points for her journal.

Thursday, July 14
"Nothing spectacular happened, but felt God's presence."

Missionaries have more than one occupation. This truth shows up in the nomenclature. Missionary doctor. Missionary nurse. Missionary teacher. Missionary translator. Even missionaries not serving in an ecclesial office are servant leaders in the church. Sunday is an important workday for missionaries. Worship is the primary task of the church, and missionaries in places like Nasir must become worship leaders. For all pastors and worship leaders everywhere, Sunday is not really a Sabbath; therefore, they need an alternate day as their primary day of rest. Years before Arlene arrived at Nasir, the medical staff had chosen Thursday as their day of rest, so on that day the clinic was closed.

On this Thursday, Arlene joined the morning prayers for an hour and a half. Then she followed the normal routine of planning meals and assisting the household staff. However, she took the day off from language lessons, allowing some time for reflection. Here she was in Africa, away from family but very much at home. God had led her here, she was sure of it. She was happy and surprisingly without fear here. She had grown up in a protective environment—her tribe looked down the Iowa road and issued consistent warnings. Her Grandma Schuiteman, Pa's mother, was a standard-bearer of worry, especially regarding disease. She was from the pre-penicillin generation that had witnessed the devastation of the influenza epidemic at the end of World War I. She had grown up in a time when a simple infection could take a life.

While Pa had not inherited his mother's spirit of fear, he was still a careful man. For example, he taught his girls to run for the house when they heard the jingle of the bells on his team of horses.

He suspected he did not have the strength to rein in the horses when they wanted to get to the water trough at the end of a long plowing day, so he taught the girls to think ahead and be safe.

In like fashion, Ma anticipated dangers and taught her girls to avoid them. The farmhouse was close to the railroad track, and hoboes who rode the rails jumped down to walk through the field and beg a meal. Ma often had a plate ready, but she taught the girls to stay out of sight. None of the men roaming past the farm during the Great Depression ever harmed a Schuiteman woman, but Ma said she would rather be safe than sorry.

Safe. That is what Arlene felt on this Thursday, alone in a house in a village in the Sudan. And safe felt like the nearness of God.

Friday, July 15
"Lul has completed 1st transaction for 2nd wife!"

Arlene had language lessons nearly every day for several hours. Several tutors, often called "informants," worked with her. Gatleak. Gat Wec. Ruan. Language lessons included talking in Nuer, which had to be about something. So, along with Nuer words, Arlene got the local news. Today's news was that a deal had been struck and the first cows had been paid. Lul could begin the consummation of his second marriage. Arlene did not feel joy. She missed Marian and felt in her heart that another brick had been laid in the wall enclosing the women of this culture.

Saturday, July 16
"Changing two to cow's milk."

The switch to cow's milk had immediately helped Arlene's smallest patient. The news of this success spread, and Arlene had two more babies to see this Saturday.

With the success of her premie, Arlene decided to put two more infants on cow's milk rather than the powdered formula. There was, however, an immediate challenge to the cow's milk solution: Arlene could no longer keep a supply of bacteria-free milk on hand, because the house refrigerator had broken down. She asked the house cooks to purchase milk at the *suk* or from one of the merchants who passed by daily. She put a system in place, instructing a member of each baby's family to return twice daily, morning and evening, to pick up a fresh supply of properly pasteurized milk. In addition, the family members were asked to bring their babies back the next Saturday to be weighed.

The word continued to spread. As the small babies grew, the number of babies in Arlene's care grew. Arlene had high hopes that her dream to improve the infant mortality rate could be reached.

Sunday, July 17
"Refrige still not working right."

The large, white upright refrigerator at the mission station in Nasir was run by kerosene, which fed a burning wick in the lower part of the unit, and the heat coming from the wick controlled the chemical mixture that provided the cooling effect. Like any refrigerator, this one could run too warm or too icy. Care had to be taken to trim the wick regularly and correctly. If the wick was cut too low, it would go out. If the wick was set too high, it would burn hot, sending smoke and even sparks up the chimney at the back of the fridge.

Some missionaries would not be without a refrigerator. Even some who believed in housing themselves in the manner of the locals required a fridge. Arlene knew of one missionary family who moved a kerosene refrigerator into a Sudan-style grass hut. It seemed like a good idea until a spark went up the chimney and the roof caught fire.

Arlene, on the other hand, would not normally have been overly concerned that the refrigerator at the mission house was indisposed. After all, she had grown up without a fridge at the farm. Here, however, she needed the cooling machine for medical purposes. She had been relying on it to keep milk on hand for her babies project, and she was also experimenting with ice to treat scorpion bites. Although scorpion bites were not fatal, they tended to be very painful for the first twenty-four hours. Arlene didn't have access to topical anesthetics, and at this time of year, she had many patients in distress over bites. Scorpions tended to come inside out of the rain, and most Nuer did not wear shoes. Arlene had discovered that a little ice administered for a short time could be a great help.

Arlene had done her best to keep the refrigerator's wick properly trimmed, but now there was some other problem with the fridge. Another day, another challenge.

Monday, July 18
"Expecting Marian, but she didn't come."

A steamboat was expected.

The steamboat almost always brought something for the missionaries—letters, packages, supplies, news, and sometimes people. Several clues hinted at a steamboat's imminent arrival. Runners brought word as to where the boat was last seen. The postmaster may have received a cable about the boat's location. A puff of smoke seen across many miles of flat grassland was a dependable sign. The chug of the engine could also be heard from some distance. An especially eager person might carry binoculars to the top of the windmill to catch the first glimpse of the next steamboat on the Sobat.

In the absence of her roommates, Arlene had enjoyed her days of solitude in the house. She continued to work at her language lessons, sneaking away on breaks to do some nursing. In the evenings, she visited with the Nuer and with the Gordons. She reflected and prayed. The truth, however, was that she missed Marian and looked forward to her return. Marian was a seasoned missionary with a

passionate heart for the things of God. In her most recent update
to the mission stations in the surrounding area, Marian had closed
with these words:

> *The big things we feel we need—as a mission compound and as*
> *a much larger community—a deeper working of His spirit (to*
> *see our sin for what it is) and to have a desire to be renewed.*

This was the Marian Arlene was eager to embrace when the
next steamboat arrived.

Tuesday, July 19
"Mail came!!"

The *Nakehlia* came puffing and chugging in with the dawn.
Marian stepped off, tired but in good condition and glad to be home.

Later that morning, after the steamship's supply of mail had
been carted to the post office, a postman came to the front of the
house, clapping his hands for attention. Ushered onto the veranda,
he dumped open his sack of mail addressed to anyone at the mission station. It was a huge pile, and everyone dropped to the floor to
help sort it all out. Arlene's bounty was forty-three letters and two
packages. Her tactic was to sort the letters by date and then spend
every available moment reading. These letters were an outpouring
of love and news from afar. Arlene sometimes said that mail day
gave her emotional indigestion, but she felt a responsibility to answer each letter—so she feasted.

Wednesday, July 20
"Looked at slides."

Arlene and Marian invited the Gordon family over for Mrs.
Gordon's birthday. During the party, there was another downpour.
While the Gordons waited for a break in the rain before taking the
children home, Arlene suggested they look at some slides of her

family and farm that she had brought from Sioux Center—which they did, holding the little squares up to the lantern.

Since leaving home, Arlene had taken plenty more pictures with her Argus C3, but there was no way to develop them here. Arlene wrote to her parents, "Our camera shop on 5th Avenue in Nasir isn't much to brag about!!! In fact, it is nothing to look at. In fact, it is nothing." She kept careful record of each photo she took and mailed each roll of film home, along with the descriptions of what they contained. Arlene would not see those particular slides until years later.

Thursday, July 21
"Mob of [patients] at clinic with little help."

The day before, Dr. Gordon had spent much of the day ferrying a fellow missionary toward Akobo in the motorboat, and a large rain in the afternoon had kept the normal Wednesday afternoon patients away.

As Thursday was not usually a clinic day, the dressers were not around. The patients, who had stayed out of the rain the day before, were now desperate to see the doctor, so Dr. Gordon opened the clinic—and Arlene cancelled her language lessons. On a normal clinic day, two hundred patients could be expected. Today there were many more.

If the clinic was open twenty-four hours a day, then there would be patients around the clock. One of the challenges for the staff at the Nasir clinic was to learn how to close the door in the face of constant human suffering.

After a dreadfully long day's work, the missionaries had supper, followed by their usual Thursday evening prayer meeting. Then Arlene lit the lamp and typed, including a letter to her folks asking if her sister Harriet's baby had been born. News travels slowly by steamship. Unbeknownst to Arlene, her niece, Arlys Ann, had been in the world already for seven days.

Friday, July 22
"Usual care of tukl *pts."*

A collection of grass huts stood solemnly about fifty yards from the clinic. These were classic grass-roofed *tukls* but with Western-style wooden doors that could close out sound, rain, and even people when privacy was needed. These huts were for patients convalescing during a more protracted illness or healing process. In other words, these *tukls* were Nasir's hospital rooms.

There was no such thing as a hospital cafeteria. Inpatients would be accompanied by family members, who would sleep outside the *tukl* and cook food for themselves and the patient. Relatives would provide personal care, while Arlene and one of the dressers would make rounds checking vitals, administering medicine, and sending for the doctor if necessary.

Arlene tried to make things as comfortable as possible in the hospital *tukls*, but patients in Nuerland did not want to spend a night in a clinic *tukl* any more than patients anywhere want to be in the hospital. Of course, some needed specialized attention for a time. Typical patients were recovering from surgery. Other common conditions were malaria, yaws (a nonvenereal form of syphilis), pneumonia, worms, whooping cough, snakebite, broken bones, and Nuerland's great enemy—tuberculosis (TB).

The missionary doctors needed outside help to definitively diagnose TB. Dr. Gordon had sent a young man named Cieng Piŋ (pronounced "Chung Ping") to Malakal to have his lungs X-rayed because he had been coughing up frothy blood by the cupful. Cieng Piŋ had traveled back with Marian on the *Nakehlia*, and the X-rays he brought back with him confirmed that he had TB in both lungs.

Cieng Piŋ was a Christian who had attended the government school and knew English quite well. Arlene was easily able to communicate to him that he would need to remain in a clinic *tukl* for a very long time.

Saturday, July 23
"Babies not gaining wt!"

The day arrived for the babies to be brought for weighing. Arlene's hopes were dashed. The cow's milk was no longer working—and neither had the powdered milk! How much longer could these children survive without proper sustenance? Arlene told the family members that she wished to see their babies again in three days. She prayed they would be returned alive.

Sunday, July 24
"Gac's cow was lost."

When Gac awoke that morning, one of his cows was missing.

Today was Gac's Sunday to cook for Arlene and her roommates, but he sent word that he was not coming. He would need to spend the day trying to find his cow—for as long as it took.

Arlene understood immediately. There was nothing so important to the Nuer as their cattle. The Nuer man knows each cow by name, description, and lineage. His cows are his greatest treasure, and Gac's cow would be found. The neighbors would join the search—for as long as it took.

Arlene and Marian would tend to their own meals today. Of greater urgency were the babies. Arlene would purchase and boil the milk, prepare and distribute each bottle, morning and evening. The usual church duties would continue, and the *tukl* patients would be cared for. Although Arlene was sure that the lost cow had no ill intent, this Sunday was certainly not a day of rest.

Monday, July 25
"The Tamai and Nuer both came in."

Late Monday afternoon two steamboats arrived, one following the other. This was not a fluke of scheduling but rather a response to great need. The dura crop was not yet mature, and due to a weak harvest the previous season, the Nuer were going hungry. The need for grain was so great that the government had set up a rationing system. Now they were releasing some extra grain because of the need in the south. The grain would be unloaded at Nasir, and those who could afford grain would eat.

Arlene faced beggars every day. She wrote to her youngest sister, Milly:

We can't begin to feed all of them, and it isn't easy to turn them away. These people eat only two meals a day normally but now they sometimes go without food for a couple days.

"Give to those who ask," Jesus had said. Jesus' words seemed straightforward and easy to follow—but not today.

Tuesday, July 26
"Changed back to Cow's and Gates."

The babies were weighed again, and they were still not gaining. Arlene knew she must narrow the factors of this medical mystery and that she needed to act quickly.

Her first premie had done well on pasteurized milk from Arlene's own fridge. She knew it was good milk because she had been drinking it herself. She had no lactometer, but she was a farm girl and knew what good cow milk tasted like. The milk, however, had stopped working when they bought it from roaming milk merchants.

Dr. Gordon wasn't surprised. He told Arlene about the time a merchant came by with a small tin of milk for sale. When they poured the milk through a cloth to strain it, a number of small minnows were seen flopping in the strainer.

The cook said to the merchant, "You put river water in the milk to fill up the tin!"

The merchant was nonplussed. "Well, don't the cows drink water from the river?"

Arlene made a guess that she'd been distributing milk that provided little more sustenance than water. She decided to switch all the babies to "Cows and Gates"—the powdered milk that came in orange tins purchased in Malakal. But she needed to make this switch with care and then make sure the children actually received the formula. She was well aware that Nuer patients sometimes used their medicines in an unorthodox manner. A patient might be given a pill to swallow in the morning and sent home with additional pills to take later. The patient, not wishing to be selfish, would simply hang the pills from the rafters of the house, expecting that they were somehow providing health to everyone who entered the house, including themselves. Arlene imagined *tukls* throughout the countryside with bags of powdered baby formula hanging from the rafters.

She knew what she would do. She would mix the formula herself and require it be picked up every morning and every evening. She would give strict instructions that the bottle not be opened but fed immediately to the infant upon arriving home.

Wednesday, July 27
"Gac's nephew bitten by cobra gave serum."

A shout, a cry, and then a running call were heard coming down the path. There would be no polite clapping of the hands at the door, only a continuing commotion.

Gac, their cook, had been away from work looking for his lost cow. Now he came running back, carrying his ten-year-old nephew to Dr. Gordon. The naked child was shaking all over. His closed eyes were puffed up, and even though his body was thrashing, he was nonresponsive. Although he had been bitten only minutes earlier, he had less than an hour to live unless something was done. Arlene assisted as Dr. Gordon administered two ampules of anti-snakebite serum. The serum was expensive, but Dr. Gordon tried to make sure there was always some on hand.

The red cobra was the deadliest of the venomous snakes in eastern Africa. One could not avoid them completely. Once, as Arlene was walking to church, she looked up at the sky. Marian, five paces behind her, suddenly rasped, "Arlene!" Arlene turned to see a cobra raised and ready. She had stepped right over it. Arlene quickly relearned the proverb, Ponder the path of your feet.

The boy's body calmed and he descended into a coma. The snake had bitten high on the boy's thigh, and those who understood the body's circulatory system had little hope that the poison had been stopped in time. Now came the waiting.

Thursday, July 28
"XX"

Once a month, double Xs showed up in Arlene's journal. Like women around the world, she made note of her monthly cycle. Arlene had an extra commonality with Nuer women concerning menstruation. For both Dutch and Nuer cultures, a menstruating woman was regarded with superstition. For the Nuer woman, menstruation meant she was not to be touched, especially not by a man. She was not to have anything to do with a cow, as her blood flow was considered harmful to cattle. She was not to visit the cattle area, drink milk, or eat food from a kettle used to boil milk. She was to stay inside her *tukl* during those days, sitting on ashes to absorb the flow. She was unclean.

For the Dutch of Arlene's mother's generation, a menstruating woman was not untouchable, but there was one odd superstition that prevailed, even among the twentieth-century Christians of northwest Iowa. Every so often, Pa killed a fatted calf and a steer. They were drained of their blood in the shed, and then Pa skinned and quartered the animals, bringing the meat portions into the kitchen to be sectioned and canned by Ma and Aunt Gert. When butchering day approached, Pa checked with Ma to be certain her monthly cycle would not be occurring that day. Likewise, Ma coordinated with Gert. They were guided by an old Dutch belief that the touch of a menstruating woman would cause fresh meat to spoil.

In Nuer culture, as untouchable as a menstruating woman was, there was an even greater fear about touching a dead person. If you touched the skin of a dead person, a whole series of rituals must ensue to cleanse you of your sin. If a person died while in your care, you must not touch them but immediately turn away.

Gac's nephew remained comatose but still alive. On this day, Arlene touched him, unafraid for either him or herself.

Friday, July 29
"I asked Cieng Piŋ to help me."

As neither Gatleak nor Gat Wec came for language lessons, Arlene asked Cieng Piŋ if he felt strong enough to give her a language lesson. He agreed as long as she would return the favor by reading to him in English from the Bible. He was already a Christian but admitted to slipping away from his faith. He was glad that this disease of TB had brought him back among Christians.

Cieng Piŋ had spent a year studying at the Mundri Teacher's Training school, a high school in the deep south. He had no interest in returning to the rural life of the people. He hoped to go to university someday, if he could survive.

Cieng Piŋ had no money, and his family did not travel to Nasir to take care of him. He depended upon the kindness of the mission. Arlene wondered if he would be able to stand living in a clinic *tukl* for the recuperation time that would be necessary, which could be as long as a year.

In a neighboring clinic *tukl*, Gac's nephew emerged from his coma. This was a surprise, and the day ended with great rejoicing.

Saturday, July 30
"The babies all looking fine."

The last Saturday of the month was also a day of joy. The strict powdered milk strategy had worked. The babies had all gained weight!

(Leap forward sixty years to April 2015. Arlene is leaving a Nuer wedding in Omaha, Nebraska, when a tall man approaches and asks, "Nya BiGoaa?"

"Yes."

"My name is Chole Gat Luak. Thank you."

"What for?"

"I was one of your babies. The ones you prepared food for every day. You kept me alive. I was wondering . . . did you happen to take any pictures?")

Sunday, July 31
"So tired."

This Sabbath day turned out to be a day of conflict, external and internal. The early morning Bible study became an argument over the Kuoth brothers—members of the church who were following the path of polygamy. Vandy had written this suggestion to Arlene: "You might call in the men and make an issue out of this by asking them what the Lord says and if they mean to take a stand." Arlene had not done as Vandy suggested. It was more in Arlene's style to pray and wait. The men had raised the question on their own, and the conversation had been contentious with no definitive conclusion.

Later in the day, Arlene experienced more tension in the clinic. Even though the clinic was closed, an Arab woman insisted on a medical procedure. Arlene agreed to help, but she found herself nursing a growing prejudice. In her experience thus far, the local Arab women were demanding. Arab culture, at least in Nasir, seemed to set itself as superior to the Nuer culture. Arlene knew that her impression was a generalization and therefore wrong, but time and again she observed an Arab unwillingness to wait their turn. Arabs arrived at the clinic in groups, seldom interacted with the Nuer, never sat down near the Nuer, and loudly insisted that their conditions required immediate attention. Such behavior was effective, since Dr. Gordon and Arlene found that they kept the peace if they attended to Arabs immediately. Otherwise, everyone was in for a long, loud, impatient, angry persistence. The Nuer also persisted, but their technique was to poke a finger into your shoulder and then gently drag that finger down the upper arm. The impatient Nuer person would repeat this action over and over. A Nasir medical professional learned to work while ignoring a Nuer finger poke.

Arlene's reserves were drained. Maybe it was emotional strain, or perhaps it was physical. She had been taking her malaria medication faithfully, but she felt a little nauseous, a little feverish, and she ached in every joint.

Arlene stayed on her feet. She prepared the bottles of formula for the babies. That evening on the veranda, she joined some other mission staff members for a Bible study. Accompanied by the occasional splash of a fish in the Sobat just steps away, Marian led a discussion of Romans 8:

> *I am persuaded, that neither death, nor life,*
> *nor angels, nor principalities, nor powers,*
> *nor things present, nor things to come,*
> *nor height, nor depth,*
> *nor any other creature,*
> *shall be able to separate us from the love of God,*
> *which is in Christ Jesus our Lord.*

8

Night in the Village

Wed. Claustrophobia at 2 A.M. Hard rain
from 3–8. Beds got wet and moved into hut.

August 17, 1955

The daily rains grew weaker, and the mission boarding school took its midterm break. Marian's boarding school students went home for two weeks, so she decided to visit one of her older students who lived in a village at some distance from Nasir. She intended to ask the village elders for permission to have that young woman teach girls in that village who were not yet attending school. Marian was a pioneer and visionary who consistently sought after equal education for females in the Sudan.

Traveling out to the villages was old stuff to Marian. Take the boat downriver. Haul along a cot, a bedroll, and enough food to spend the night. Return the next day. She asked Arlene to go along, as company would turn the trip from old stuff into an adventure. Arlene readily agreed.

As Marian checked things over for the trip, the boat's motor misbehaved. She fussed over it and got it working well enough. After lunch in Nasir, the two adventurers filled the motorboat with supplies, including a camp stove, fresh water, and enough food to be away overnight. Arlene took her medical kit, and, as always, a book to read. When Marian pulled the rope, the motor started, not with a roar but a continuing cough. One of the spark plugs was not catching. Over the hack of the engine, Marian said, "It'll smooth out as we go. We'll get five horsepower instead of ten—it'll just be slow for a while."

Marian was the senior missionary, having been here for a decade, and was an experienced boater. As it was in Arlene's nature to say, "Let's try," she smiled and nodded, and off they went.

They putt-putted at slow speed for a few miles, but there was no "smoothing out." Marian pushed the kill switch and let the boat drift. She dug out the toolkit, and she and Arlene took off the engine cover and pulled out the spark plugs. Nothing obvious was amiss. They looked things over a bit, but since neither of them was a mechanic, they were only able to confirm that it looked complicated.

Marian laid out some options. They could go right back—or they could go for an afternoon's visit to a closer village where she had been to preach. Arlene liked that idea, since some of her formula babies were from that village, and she would like to examine them in their natural surroundings.

Arlene or Marian—it could have been either one—said, "Let's pray." They did, asking for help in discerning whether they should turn back before evening.

Marian put the plugs back in and then pulled the rope. The motor lumbered to its feet, but sounded as if it had tuberculosis. Marian guided the boat to the Wako (a tributary of the Sobat) and turned. The vessel sputtered its way to the closest village, called Dhik Dhik, where the two missionaries enjoyed a visit with their acquaintances there. Back at the boat, the sickly motor staggered further up the Wako, spitting all the way. Having come this far, Marian and Arlene decided to attempt their destination village by nightfall. They turned up a *khor* (a nameless tributary), trying to find their way to the far village. Then the motor began to smoke. Marian killed it to let it cool off.

Seated in the boat down in the *khor*, they could not see the lay of the land. Truly, there was not much to be seen out here. There were matching grass-roofed *tukls* scattered across the swamps, and an occasional small tree, but that was all you saw. It all looked the same unless you knew what you were looking for.

A man came to the edge of the *khor* and raised his chin to look over the reeds. Marian conversed with him briefly in Nuer and then began setting up the camp stove in the bottom of the boat.

"What did you say?" Arlene asked her.

"I asked him where we were."

"What did he say?"

"I'm not sure. So I asked him if he knew a place we could spend the night. He said we can stay in their *kaal* [farmyard]. I told him we'd have our supper in the boat first and then decide."

By now, it was about an hour before nightfall, when it would suddenly get very dark. Walking up to the *kaal* in the dark would be foolish since they could not see the snakes, scorpions, leopards, hyenas, and crocodiles that were more adept at moving about in the dark than any human. Arlene sprang into action, pulling out sandwiches, tomatoes, peppers, and lemonade while Marian heated some soup on the camp stove. At this point, there were more eyes peering at them through the reeds. Marian, a nonstop talker, chattered away in Nuer to the onlookers in the reeds. Arlene smiled and waved.

After supper, the motor had cooled down, so they decided to try to make it back to the Sobat and go home. Pull. Nothing. Pull. Nothing. With each pull, the sun went down a little further. After "One more try," they gave up. They moved the boat, using the paddle and pulling on the undergrowth, getting it as far into the reeds as it would go. Grabbing their cots, bedrolls, jungle hammocks, and rifles, they left everything else in the boat and slogged up the low embankment, through the swampland onto higher ground.

The *kaal* stood at a short distance. Evening cow gathering was underway. The man and his boys were moving the cattle into the large barn that stood between the separate *tukls* where each of the man's wives slept with her respective children.

As the swamp gave way to the slightly higher-ground *kaal*, Marian and Arlene had to watch where they walked even more than before. Most of the *kaal* was filled with cow pies, which are certainly not waste to the Nuer. Manure was useful for fuel, fertilizer, and decorating the body and hair for fancy occasions like a wedding dance.

The dark closed in, and so did the mosquitos. Time was of the essence. Marian greeted the farmer, his wives, and their children while Arlene found a spot near one of the women's huts to set up their cots. These raised, portable beds protected them from the manure, the mud, and the snakes. Having spread their bedrolls out on the cots, the next step was to tie up the jungle hammocks. Arlene had purchased two jungle hammocks at an Army Surplus store back in Sioux City and packed them both into the barrels her Uncle Ed had shipped for her. There is no jungle, however, in the south Sudan. There is swamp, tall grass, and small trees. In a permanent, higher ground settlement such as Nasir, trees can grow older and larger, but that was the exception. Nevertheless, Arlene and Marian were glad to have these jungle hammocks with them now. They hung the hammocks over their cots to create a canvas roof that would keep off the rain. Mosquito netting fell from the sides of the canvas roof and encircled the cots below. Makeshift but marvelous.

Marian and Arlene zipped themselves into their protective netting while the Nuer reached into their cooling fires, grabbing handfuls of warm ash to rub on their bodies to ward off the marauding insects. It was nighttime in Nuerland.

One could feel very alone in this dark, especially after the cooking fires died down. The huts were close by, however, and after a while, the man asked a question and Marian answered. Even though Arlene had been studying Nuer now for many weeks, she understood little of the conversation. She did catch the word *Kuoth*, which she knew meant "God."

Marian and the man were talking about God. What did they say?

Marian later tried to reconstruct the conversation, recalling that the man asked questions about God she had not been asked before.

"Do you women have a husband?" he had asked.

"No, Father," Marian had replied.

"Do you have your own cows?"

"We do not have cows."

"You are waiting to get cows as a marriage price?"

"We might not get married."

"How will you get children?"

"Our job is to help all children."

"But who will help you when you are old?"

"We believe that *Kuoth Chaka* will take care of us."

"Ah, *Kuoth Chaka*. The creator of the People. I sacrifice to this God. How do you make your sacrifices if you have no husband and no cows?"

"We do not make sacrifices."

"Then *Kuoth Chaka* will not take care of you."

"*Kuoth Chaka*'s son has made a sacrifice for us."

"*Kuoth Chaka* has a son?"

"*Awhn.*"

"Who is *Kuoth Chaka*'s son?"

"*Jeethuth.*" The Nuer language does not have an "s" sound, so the name "Jesus" becomes *Jeethuth* (or *Jeebuth*) in Nuer.

"*Jeethuth?*"

"*Awhn.*"

"*Jeethuth* has cows?"

"*Jeethuth* did not use cows for sacrificing. He sacrificed with his own body."

"He killed himself?"

"He did not kill himself."

"Then he did not make a true sacrifice."

"He did die. But others killed him."

Sometimes there was silence in the conversation.

"I would kill anyone who kills my son. Did *Kuoth Chaka* kill the men who killed his son?"

"*Jeethuth* asked *Kuoth Chaka* not to kill them. *Jeethuth* asked his father to forgive them and to take them into his family."

"Even if my son asked me, I could not stop myself from killing them. And I would never take my son's killers into my family."

"Yes. Only God has that much strength."

"*Awhn*, my daughter. *Kuoth Chaka* is a strong God. *E rach mi guaa* [It is good talk]."

There was silence for a bit, and then the man spoke again, "I could not leave it alone if my son was killed."

Marian laughed. "Oh, of course! *Kuoth Chaka* could not leave it alone either. He did not kill his son's killers, but instead he brought *Jeethuth* back to life."

The man laughed. "*Kuoth Chaka* did that? I have not heard of a god or man who could do that."

"*Kuoth Chaka* did. He brought his son back to life. And he forgave his son's killers. And he told the killers they could live in his *tukl* if they wished. Do you know who they are?"

"Who?"

"The ones who killed *Jeethuth*."

"No, I do not."

"Everyone did it. Even me. Even my friend, Arlene. Everyone."

"No, not everyone. I did not do it."

"We did not do it with our hands. Other people did it with their hands. But all of us did it with our hearts. Even you, Father."

"I did not do that. Even in my heart."

"Father, I am sorry. I do not know what is in your heart. But you know. And *Kuoth Chaka* knows. And he asked me to tell you that he forgives you because of the sacrifice his son made."

"He asked you to tell me?"

"He wrote it in a letter."

"You have received a writing from *Kuoth Chaka*?"

"It is not written in your language. But my friend *Nyarial* is putting it into the words of the People."

"I would like to hear this letter."

"Can you come to the town of Nasir?"

"I do not go to the town unless I get sick. But I will think about this talk."

"Thank you, Father. May I speak of you in my prayers to *Kuoth Chaka*?"

"*Awhn.*"

At 2:00 a.m., Arlene awakened. Clouds covered the sky. There was no light anywhere. She felt closed in, trapped.

"Marian?" she called.

Silence.

"Marian!"

"I'm right here."

"I think I need to get up."

"If you need to use the bathroom, it's anywhere you like."

"No. I feel trapped. Can you walk around with me?"

"Oh. Yes. Sure."

The two of them unzipped their netting and reached for each other in the darkness. After a short while, Arlene said she was ready to try to get back to sleep. Marian whispered a prayer, and Arlene fell quickly to sleep.

Then the *luth ruun* (the heavy rain) began to fall. Normally, they loved a *luth ruun* because everyone stayed inside and slept in. It was a wonderful feeling back in Nasir. Here in the *kaal*, however, the rain was so heavy that the jungle hammocks filled with water and sagged down onto the sleeping women. Arlene awakened at 3:00 with nowhere to move. If she tried to get up, the water would spill onto the cot. In spite of feeling more trapped than ever, she stayed put until 5:30 when the roofs of the jungle hammocks began to leak. Both women got up and slipped into one of the huts, where they were readily welcomed and treated as special guests. They dozed on the earthen floor. After three more hours, the rain finally stopped. One of the babies in the hut was fussing, and Arlene discovered an eye infection, which she treated from her medicine kit, leaving enough medicine for later.

Saying their goodbyes, the women returned, soaked and mud-caked, to the boat. They pulled on the starter rope until their hands blistered, but the motor would not catch. There was nothing to do now but row. Arlene paddled while Marian cooked breakfast. After fifteen minutes, they switched. At times it rained, so they bailed and rowed, and when the skies cleared, one of them read aloud while the other rowed.

They made it to the mouth of the Wako and turned upstream, breaking into songs of praise and prayers. They prayed throughout the morning, a longer than usual prayer service in which they were able to name many more people and concerns than in their usual prayer meetings at Nasir. It was a deeply satisfying and memorable time of intercession and gratitude.

At noon, they moored in the reeds so they could eat their lunch without getting pushed back downstream. Then the wind came up and the current grew strong. They no longer made headway by paddling alone, so they stayed close to shore and pulled themselves along by grabbing reeds. By midafternoon, they came to a village at last and hired two men to paddle the boat home. To lighten the load, Marian and Arlene got out and walked the last several miles through deep swamp water and mud, arriving at dusk, just as Bob and Vi were sending out rowers to look for them.

The adventurers cleaned up, got some supper, and collapsed into bed. Early the next morning, they could hear someone fussing with the boat motor. Fellow missionaries, Verne and Lorraine Sikkema, had arrived. Verne was an excellent mechanic and within a short while, he had the boat operating good as new.

Later, Arlene wondered whether they had misunderstood the answer to their prayers about turning back. Or maybe all the trouble was so they would spend the night in the *kaal* where Marian could have that conversation with the man about the gospel. Maybe it was so the two women could have the unusually long and sweet time of prayer while paddling home. Maybe it was to bind their friendship through experience and memory making. Or maybe not everything has a reason. Maybe some reasons are known only to *Kuoth Chaka* and held as close and dark as a cloud-filled African village night.

9

I Am a Dog

*Wed. 4 hrs language. Worked in clinic medicine room.
Nya Top, Dwir's wife, clapped. Baby with cleft palate
died in P.M. Marian and I took jeep toward forest.*

November 23, 1955

Vandy was still gone from Nasir. Before she left, she had asked Nya Top to speak regularly with Arlene. Vandy was eager for Nya Top to provide Arlene with ongoing Nuer language practice, and Nya Top would force the issue since she did not know English. Vandy also knew that Nya Top had her own need for friendship.

Nya Top was not from Nasir. She was living away from home. "Home" itself is a complex notion for the Nuer since the People have for millennia lived a nomadic life, migrating at least twice a year as dictated by the rains, the rise and fall of the river, and the needs of their cattle. Home is where the cows are.

Nya Top was not living according to the rhythms of rain, river, and cows. She, her husband, and children had settled into a clinic *tukl*. Indefinitely. Nya Top's husband, whose name was Dwir Biliew, was a patient of sorts. He was at the clinic because of psychological problems. There was no psychiatrist, however, so Dwir was a long-term patient. This meant that Nya Top and the children were long-term residents as well.

Dwir's condition was difficult to assess. He seemed capable of work, but the mission's attempts to assign him tasks around the compound were not always successful. It was not clear whether his disconnect was a matter of culture or common sense. For example, someone asked him to "make the beds." He took the sheets off, rolled them, and placed them on the end of the bed. He was handling the sheets as one would handle a grass mat in a *tukl*. Certainly, he was a man of village life and not used to the ways of Western culture.

Dwir's difficulties extended to his social interactions. When working for the mission, he attended daily clinic staff devotions. Partway through one meeting, he walked over to Arlene and embraced her. This gesture would have been fine, except that he held the embrace too long—and Dwir wore only a white cloth flung over his shoulder. Reet, one of the clinic dressers, took Dwir by the hand and led him back to his *tukl*, and then Arlene excused herself and went home.

Arlene's friendship with Dwir's wife was not harmed by the strange embrace. Arlene and Nya Top did not even speak about the incident, but then they struggled to speak at all. Their conversations were limited to nouns and verbs rather than emotional descriptors such as "frightened" and "hurt." But they read each other's eyes. They held the same children. They smiled. They endured a common shame.

Though Dwir seemed incapable of being an adequate husband to Nya Top, she was a wife to him. The day before Thanksgiving, Nya Top bore another child, squatting on the hardened earthen floor of the clinic *tukl*. She left the baby in the care of her husband, and, typical of a Sudanese woman, took matters relating to her children into her own hands. She walked to the clinic veranda and clapped her hands. This baby was different; she needed the doctor.

Dr. Gordon followed Nya Top Biliew back to the *tukl*. After seeing the baby, he sent a runner with a note for Arlene:

> *The Biliew baby was born with a cleft palate. I'm going to need help. Be thinking about how to care for her. Come and see me after your siesta.*

Dr. Gordon knew Arlene was probably lying down for the usual afternoon rest time everyone took to get out of the midday hundred-degree heat.

Arlene knew something about a cleft palate, sometimes called a harelip at that time. Technically, cleft palate and cleft lip are two separate conditions. Nya Top's baby seems to have been born with both. Not only had Arlene studied these anomalies in school, but also Arlene's Aunt Gert, Ma's sister, had been born with them. Arlene's Grandpa Rozeboom had taken his daughter Gert to Milwaukee in the late 1800s for a series of operations. The doctoring gave Gert a long and meaningful life, but there was not the level of plastic surgery available today. Gert's classmates were untrained in how to respond to persons with a disability, and when Gert was growing up, children with physical disabilities tended to be sequestered. Some children were literally locked away in the upstairs of a house. A sentence such as "They have a child locked in the bedroom" could pass by in a conversation without comment.

Gert moved about freely, however, which was an indication of her father's love and of Gert's own courage. She never hid her face, and her classmates rewarded her by calling her *Oliphanta*, Dutch for "elephant."

Gert never married. It was typical in her era that one child in every household was chosen (whether openly or tacitly) to care for the parents in their waning years, and if that child was a woman, she commonly remained unmarried. Gert seemed destined for the task. Her father lived to be an old man, and Gert cared for him until he died in the house he had built on 1st Avenue in Sioux Center.

Arlene immediately thought of her Aunt Gert when Bob's note arrived. The memory of Aunt Gert gave Arlene a surge of hope, but then it faded. Gert had Milwaukee. Nya Top's baby had only here. There might be the possibility of surgery in Khartoum, but keeping the child alive for such a journey was doubtful. Without a palate, the baby would not be able to suck. A feeding tube might be possible, but even with great care, this procedure came with the likelihood of sores and infection.

At 2:00, Arlene went to visit the baby. Dwir came out of the *tukl*, but neither the mother nor the child was present. Dwir pointed away from the river toward the thorn trees. Was there a native medicine man living in the scrub forest, or had the child already died? Dwir shrugged. To him, it was the mother's business.

Arlene walked around, calling for Nya Top. She found her by the river, throwing dust on her head and muttering, "*Ean cetke jiok* [I am a dog]." Nya Top was in the throes of the Nuer grieving ritual. The child was gone. The child would not be back. The child was dead.

Nya Top was expressing not only terrible grief but also shame. What was she blaming herself for? Nuer culture suggests several possible reasons. First, some Nuer thought that infant mortality indicated unfaithfulness on the part of the mother. Arlene doubted that anyone would claim such a thing of Nya Top or that Nya Top would receive such an accusation. Nya Top had been the epitome of faithfulness. A second possibility was that the child's father had killed an elephant. A deceased elephant would seek revenge upon its killers by defacing and eventually slaying their children. Of course, Arlene did not believe in such a myth, nor did she think Dwir was capable of an elephant hunt. The third possibility was that Nya Top felt ashamed for not fulfilling the first duty of Nuer motherhood: to bring forth healthy babies and keep them alive. Nuer fathers and mothers typically placed the blame for any tragedy with an infant upon the mother's shoulders alone. There was cultural pragmatism in this approach, since if it were the Nuer father's fault, then he would need to sacrifice a cow to remove the curse. From the Nuer viewpoint, however, God was not known to hold women to so high a standard. For a mother, exacting revenge upon her child restored justice, and the additional price of a cow was not required. This, too, was cultural pragmatism since women did not own cows.

Arlene did not know whether the child had died naturally or whether one of the baby's parents had killed her. Nya Top may have carried the child alive to the thorn forest, leaving the child on the open ground to be found by beasts, or birds, or snakes.

Arlene touched Nya Top's back, a gesture that made her wail all the more. Arlene sat beside her until the sun went down. Arlene ached for the pain of her friend, and she felt ashamed for her own relief that this medical challenge was over. Although she would have done everything possible to keep the child alive, this would have been a journey of great difficulty for Arlene and Nya Top—and painful for the child. The ending, in all probability, would have been the same. A challenge arose to confront Arlene's belief in modern medicine. At what point does the application of technology, biology, and chemistry become less wise than the primitive custom of simply returning such a child to the earth?

At dusk, Arlene walked home. She knew there was little likelihood of ever knowing what happened to the child, but just to be certain, she and Marian drove the Jeep out to the thorn forest. Arlene turned off the engine, leaving the headlights on. They got out and stood for a long time, listening for a baby's cry. Then they got into the Jeep and drove home.

A year later, Nya Top would bear another child. She would name her Nya BiGoaa after Arlene.

10

Beginnings

Sun. Attended flag raising ceremony.
Sudan's independence. Mary preached.
Short nap. Alone by big tree.

January 1, 1956

Back on the first Tuesday in June 1912, a river steamer steered close to the north bank of the Sobat, not far from the *tukls* of a large Nuer village known as Kuanylualthoaan. The steamer's captain signaled to his crew to cast off the towropes of *The Evangel*, a houseboat whose engine was broken. With its ropes untied, *The Evangel* fell adrift. Tom Lambie splashed into the river to grab the boat's ropes and anchor them to the riverbank. The steamer then chugged away toward Ethiopia.

The river fell silent. Tom Lambie and his fellow missionary, the linguist E. L. McCreery, had arrived at their intended destination. They, and the Shilluk workers they had hired in Doleib Hill, lugged a tent from the deck of *The Evangel* and began pounding in stakes to establish the first Christian mission among the Nuer people. The arrival of *The Evangel* was the unofficial founding day of the American Presbyterian Mission on the Sobat River.

Lambie, a young man in his twenties, was a Pittsburgh Presbyterian with an M.D. from the University of Pennsylvania. He grabbed some medical supplies, and then Lambie and McCreery, armed with the few Nuer words they had learned in Khartoum, walked into the village to meet the people and explain why they were there. When Lambie stretched forth his hand to the village chief, the chief leaned over and spit into it, which was considered a great blessing. The missionaries were welcome and found three willing patients on their first day. By the end of the month, Dr. Lambie was caring for a hundred patients a day.

Across the river from *The Evangel* was a nearly abandoned Anglo-Egyptian military fort, known by its first district commissioner whose name was Nasser. With a doctor in the neighborhood, the military returned. Within a year, the fort had been rebuilt, but on the north side of the river. The return of the soldiers attracted merchants, a post office, a telegraph station, and the home of a British officer. The soldiers were mostly northern Sudanese and Egyptians whose language was Arabic. The merchants who provided support for the soldiers were Arabs. The town that grew outward from the base became known as Nasir, the English letters of the Arabic word for "the supporter."

By 1913, the society around the American Presbyterian Mission outpost reflected the conflict steadily building between north and south Sudan—conflict over race, religion, language, culture, and power. The American missionaries were planting their gospel seeds in thorny ground. While they could not predict the future, they set to work with honest zeal.

These tensions had existed for more than a thousand years. The Christian gospel had been brought to northern Africa by Mark, the apostle. That early missionary movement became the Coptic Church, which spread throughout Egypt and into northern Sudan. Then, in the early seventh century, Muslims conquered Egypt and soon after entered the Sudan. A fierce war ensued, finally ending in a treaty. The Sudanese government, if it could be called a government of such a large and diverse land, agreed to pay an annual tribute of slaves harvested from among its own native people, and a mosque was to be maintained for the benefit of Islamic visitors to the Sudan. The Sudanese slavery legacy continued for over a thousand years. In 1862, the British abolitionist Samuel Baker visited the Sudan and wrote that slavery "kept Khartoum going as a bustling town." More than half of Khartoum's population was slaves.

Although the British Empire invaded the Sudan in 1882 as an antislavery action, there is also the truism that empires require wealth if they are to survive. The Sudan offered such glitters as gold, emeralds, and ivory. Perhaps more important, the source waters of the Nile flowed from the southern Sudan and Sudan's coast allowed access to the Red Sea, providing military and trade route advantages. Consequently, Britain planted its rule in the Sudan, the story of which is told in the book *The River War*, penned by a young soldier named Winston Churchill.

By the turn of the last century, Great Britain agreed with Egypt to co-rule the Sudan. The arrangement was called the "Anglo-Egyptian Condominium." With this friendly government in place, American medical missionaries arrived at the mouth of the Sobat River at Doleib Hill. People were healed, and the news spread. Inland residents walked many days to reach medical care, often dying before reaching the mouth of the river. American Presbyterians sent word that they were willing to bring modern medicine to the Sudanese people who lived deeper inland.

In 1903, Lord Cromer stood before Parliament in London to encourage the British to embrace American missionary efforts to provide medical care for all of southern Sudan. The goal was to get doctors closer to the needs. The Americans hoped to establish a new mission every two hundred miles. If there was to be a mission near the swampland tribes, practicality required that the mission be along a river. When the swamps refilled each rainy season, no supplies could reach the mission except via river. From the mission's perspective, the Sobat would become a gospel highway and physical healing would be the beginning of a relationship with the region's people.

Enacting the plan took a decade, as access to south Sudan was impeded by language, culture, tribalism, and most of all the lack of roads. The rivers were the roads, and half of the year, the rivers dried, lowering to impassibility.

When the First World War weakened the British Empire, Egypt soon gained partial independence from the British Empire, quickly separating itself from sharing in the governance of the Sudan. Britain responded by creating the Sudan Defense Force to police the Sudanese countryside. The SDF's district commissioners continued to be British, but the force itself was typically Arab.

The struggle for Sudan's future was being waged not as much in the military and government as within the schools. In which language would lessons be taught? The language question was influenced by which government jobs were available to the writers of a particular language. An African proverb states that until lions have historians, the history of the hunt will glorify the hunter. The tale of southern Sudan was being written in Arabic. The south was full of local tribal people with their own unwritten languages. These people watched the boats go by. They had little money or language with which to interact with the outside world. If the military came out in force, the local tribes—men, women, and children—ran to the forest. The Nuer, through the first half of the twentieth century, were mostly content to be separatists.

The Second World War further weakened Great Britain. By the end of that war, nearly all the officers in the SDF were Sudanese from the Muslim north and the soldiers' common language was Arabic. The British had originally planned to institutionalize English as the language of a united Sudan, but the writing on the wall was in a different script.

In 1953, Britain announced its plans to leave the Sudan. Self-rule was to begin on the first day of 1956, but five months early, on August 16, 1955, the last British troops pulled out of the country.

Two days later, the Equatorial Corps of the Sudan Defense Force in the deep south mutinied, and the first of the Sudanese civil wars was underway.

At that point, Arlene had been in the country for four months.

On August 30, 1955, a telegram arrived at the mission declaring a state of emergency throughout the country. The government forbade any civilian travel.

On September 4, the *Tamai* passed through loaded with soldiers from the north. The Nuer fled to the forest. The steamboat *Nakehlia* arrived with mail, but letters had been opened and censored.

By New Year's Day 1956, things had calmed enough to stage an official celebration of Sudanese independence. A new nation was born. The missionaries were given a special invitation to come to the military flagpole early in the morning. Soldiers mounted their horses and paraded in formation. A new flag was raised. Songs were sung, and speeches were given—in Arabic. The Nasir Christians attended the early part of the celebration and then walked to the church *tukl* for morning worship. Dr. Mary Smith was in town and preached the sermon of the day—in Nuer.

That afternoon, the Nuer of nearby Kuanylualthoaan killed three cows and held an Independence Day feast. Were they hopeful about their new country? Perhaps. But Nuer seldom required much excuse to gather for dancing, drinking, and singing by the fire late into the night. Arlene could hear them as she sat alone that evening by the clinic tree, wondering what the future held, and wondering whether her tutor, Cieng Piŋ, was right when he predicted that Islamic law would one day rule the new Sudan.

11

Where's the Good?

Sun. Vandy preached (Matthew 3). Terrific sermon.
Bathed, catheterized and gave enema to patient
with CSM [cerebral spinal meningitis]. She seems
a bit better. Short trip to mouth of Wako chasing
pelicans! Revelation 6. Rapture. Am longing for it.

January 8, 1956

The day after Sudan's first Independence Day, the Missionary Aviation Fellowship plane touched down on the scorched grass runway with Vandy on board. She was returning from the mission station at Ler, where she had been stationed for half a year. The following Sunday morning, the mission's ranking Bible scholar was welcomed back into the local pulpit. Vandy's sermon text was John's desert cry, "The kingdom of heaven is at hand!" As the sun settled into the golden hour that evening, Vandy and Arlene took the boat to the mouth of the Wako near the village of Kuanylualthoaan. Turning off the engine, they drifted and watched the neighborhood pelicans make their graceful, skidding landings on the glassy water. This place, right here, right now, proclaimed the kingdom of heaven, and these women took notice. It was a typical Nasir Lord's Day coming to a grace-filled ending.

That same day, across the ocean in South America, by the time that same sun had set, two of Vandy's college friends lay on a beach, their lifeblood draining away into the sand.

Three weeks later, Arlene was busy packing for a weeklong missionary association gathering down in Akobo. She was called away to attend to a baby who had sore eyes and a burned hand. When she came back, she found her suitcase filled with all sorts of stuff: Vicks VapoRub, a kit for doing home permanents, Band-Aids, pliers, a screwdriver, a bottle of vitamins, two raincoats (even though it was the dry season), and on top, a mousetrap all set and ready to go off. Arlene had a laughing fit. Vandy replied very soberly, "I was only trying to help."

They were about to get away for a break, even if it was business related. Looking forward to a change of pace and rest, Arlene and Vandy were like children headed to the beach.

A steamship docked, one of the last of the season. The river water was draining away day by day, and the river would soon be too low for steamships to safely navigate around the sandbars. The final ships were dropping their loads and fleeing back to harbor at Khartoum. In a few hours, the mail would be delivered to the mission veranda. There would be letters to read before Arlene and the others departed for Akobo.

Returning from clinic duties that afternoon, Arlene came to her bedroom to escape the oppressive midday heat and discovered Vandy sitting there, staring vacantly with a recently arrived *Time* magazine open on her lap.

"Hi, Nyarial," Arlene said.

No answer.

"Can I see that *Time* magazine when you're done?" Arlene asked.

No answer.

"What? What is it, Vandy?"

Vandy handed Arlene the magazine, pointing to a column titled "Ecuador." The brief article told of five missionary men slain by Waodani tribesmen.

Vandy finally spoke. "Jim Elliot was my classmate at Wheaton. He and Elisabeth were in a Bible study with me. Ed McCully, too.

We were going to be missionaries and go wherever God . . . do whatever God . . ."

The missions organization at Wheaton College was one of the largest on campus, taking three pages to depict all its members in *The Tower* yearbook. These Wheaton students were of Arlene's generation, coming of age during World War II. Rather than descending into despair over the horrors of the war, they embraced a remarkable urgency, asking themselves, "If I do not help the world, who will?" They were mission-bound, zealous and committed, including a 1943 Wheaton graduate named Billy Graham.

Vandy groaned, "Where's the good, Arlene? Where is it?"

Even if Arlene had known the answer, she wisely chose silence. She just sat on the bed, reached out her arms, and enveloped her friend.

A year later, Vandy's friend, Elisabeth Elliot, would attempt an answer to Vandy's questions. In an article for *Christianity Today* titled "The Prayer of the Five Widows," she posited that all five wives had been praying for their husbands' protection, and she believed God had answered their prayers:

> *Protection from what? " . . . that thou shouldst keep them from the evil one." Each one of our five men, years before, had asked for the whole accomplishment of God's will in him at any cost, to the end that Christ be glorified. The Evil One is determined, however, that Christ shall not be glorified. But, in making them obedient men, God had answered the prayer of his Son, the prayer of the men themselves and the prayer of their wives. The adversary did not succeed in turning them aside from God's highest purpose. They were protected from that most fearful of all dangers, disobedience. They loved God above all else. "Herein is the love of God, that ye keep his commandments."*

Elisabeth went on to write a book called *Through Gates of Splendor* about her husband and the others. The book included a chapter on Roger Youderian—one of the five who died—who, facing great disappointment in the Amazon, wrote in his journal just days before his death:

> *I will die to self. I will begin to ask God to put me in a service of constant circumstances where to live to Christ, I must die to self. I will be alive unto God. That I may learn to love him with my heart, mind, soul, and body.*

Elisabeth's book made its way to Nasir. Vandy and Arlene read it, and Arlene wrote home that she especially appreciated the chapter on Youderian.

Although threat of death was not imminent for the missionaries in the Sudan, they had their own challenges. Arlene named hers "battle fatigue." Being a clinic nurse in rural Africa was so different from the way she had trained in the States. She had hundreds of patients waiting each day the clinic was open. Her veranda was a 24–7 emergency room. In addition, she was an intensive care nurse, moving among the clinic *tukls* where the desperately ill stayed for months at a time. She was also a missionary, concerned not only for the body but also for the soul. She performed her functions with limited resources, minimal experience, a language deficit, cultural barriers, and profound urgency. Each day she wondered who would die and how many.

A subtle feature of Arlene's internal landscape, however, was that she was able to distinguish disappointment from discouragement. Arlene accepted disappointment as a natural part of life. Discouragement, on the other hand, was a sin begotten of the belief that Jesus is not enough.

What would sustain Arlene in the years to come? How could she keep from being overwhelmed?

Arlene and her friends faced life's most bracing questions head-on. These were people, including Vandy's friends across the ocean in Ecuador, whose breathing in was the word of God and whose breathing out was prayer. This rhythm helped them discern what Jesus meant when he said, "If any will come after me, let them deny themselves, and take up their cross daily and follow me."

They embraced the way of the cross. What some would call a waste, they called good.

12

Nyakota's Feet

Mon. Awakened at 4:30 baby #5 with whooping cough. Then rain. Then army ants. Language lessons. Worked in clinic but didn't get any cleaning done. Letter writing and reading at night.

April 16, 1956

Arlene arrived back in Nasir after her first annual vacation to discover that a whooping cough epidemic was moving in. She could hear it coming. The sounds of the disease are hard to miss. The cough is bad enough—harsh, rasping explosions. Even more terrible is the next sound—a desperate, wheezing gasp for air that gives the disease its name. Cough, cough, cough, gasp, repeat. Infants under one year are most at risk, not only of catching the disease but also of succumbing to it. A baby with whooping cough can hardly breathe and therefore finds it difficult to eat or sleep. The condition soon leads to complications, such as pneumonia and diarrhea. The parents also lose sleep, and their hearts break as they listen to their child struggle with every breath. They pray for the sound to end, and if it suddenly does, they long to hear it once again.

In 1956, the solution to the disease was to avoid it, wait it out, or get a vaccination. Dr. Gordon had ordered the vaccine, but it had not yet arrived. Containing the disease was nearly impossible in a culture that eats with its fingers and has little concept of a microbial world.

Nyakota was the wife of Reet, one of the clinic dressers. Days after Arlene's arrival home, Nyakota bore a daughter. Arlene went to meet the newborn and examine her. She was a perfectly healthy baby, born into one of the few Christian homes. In the Nuer way, she would not be given a name until weeks later, when her life had been established. Infant mortality, after all, was at 50 percent.

A couple of weeks later, Reet preached at the Sunday service. He worked as a dresser at the clinic, he was an elder at the church, and was a respected young man from a nearby village. He looked typically Nuer in almost every way: tall and thin with six forehead *gaars* and his lower front teeth removed, as per custom. He wore an ivory bracelet shoved above his right elbow; however, he typically wore clothes because he spent much time at the clinic and at the church, where clothing was encouraged. He even wore moccasins to protect his feet, because his dresser classes had taught him of the bites and ailments easily invited by simply walking barefoot.

Reet and Nyakota were a young couple much beloved in the community, but love did not guard them from the disease that had descended upon Nasir. The week after Reet preached at church, the coughing began. Arlene and Dr. Gordon heard that slow train coming but could neither stop it nor get out of its way.

Before breakfast on Friday, April 20, Arlene and Marian heard clapping at their door. They peeked outside to see Reet and Nyakota standing there holding a small, silent bundle. Arlene easily guessed what was inside. She and Marian quickly dressed and slipped out into the cool morning air. Arlene reached out her hands and took the bundle from Nyakota. Marian drew the heartbroken mother into her own arms, and Reet asked the women to ferry them across the river. Marian knew where they would be headed, so she nodded an immediate yes. They all got into the boat.

Marian started the motor, and the somber group sailed across to the bamboo grove. After a short two hundred yards, Marian hit the kill switch and tipped the rudder slightly. Reet leaped out of the boat to pull the silver prow a few feet up the steep embankment. There was no grass on the earthen bank, but it was covered in small, dead bamboo leaves. In fact, the entire grove was covered in a thick layer of fallen brown leaves around and between clusters of bamboo spindles that arched high into the air—like the pillars of a grand, quiet cathedral.

They stood there, looking around, beginning the process of selecting a burying place. When Nyakota nodded her head, Reet knelt at her feet and spread the leaves aside. Then, with a broken piece of bamboo, he began to scrape the earth.

Soon a canoe skimmed across the river. The paddler was Gac Rik, one of the dressers who had given Arlene her Nuer name when she arrived one year ago. He saw what was happening over at the bamboo grove, and he was not going to let Reet do the digging alone.

After Gac Rik arrived, Arlene told Marian that she would be right back and went to find Kuac, their student pastor who was to be ordained later that year. Kuac came immediately and officiated one of the first funerals of his ministry.

The hole was soon completed. Nyakota cut four pieces of animal skin she had brought along, and she laid a strip of skin where the baby's head would lie and one for under her hip. She lowered the tiny corpse into its grave, resting her on her side. She covered the head and the hip with the remaining two pieces of skin, and then she and Reet covered their child in earth. When they replaced the brown leaves, there was no evidence of this burial spot—only five adults standing in a circle with bowed heads.

Normally, the grave of a Nuer infant would be marked so that the extended family could return to the grave the next day for a special ceremony. They would have in their possession the animal skin the child had slept on when alive. Standing there above the grave, the skin would be cut in half, demonstrating a final separation of the mother and child. Then the bottoms of the mother's feet would be burned. This final act of the funeral ritual guarded other children from a curse. If the mother's feet were not burned, the Nuer believed she would become an angel of death, and the youngest child of every home she entered would die.

Reet and Nyakota had decided that they would separate themselves from certain cultural practices surrounding burials. They did not believe in the mother's curse, and they would not allow Nyakota's feet to be burned. There would, however, be a price. They would become outcasts for a time, not allowed to enter the *tukls* of anyone except fellow Christians who believed as they believed. "Please pray for us," Reet said. What he meant was, *please welcome us into your homes, and if you can, please let your own feet be witnesses of the Christian way.*

Arlene thought of Isaiah 52, for which Nyakota had become a living testament: "How beautiful upon the mountains are the feet of the one who brings good news, who proclaims peace."

The Sunday after the burial of the tiny baby, Reet stood in the pulpit again and delivered the sermon. As Arlene sat in the worship *tukl* that day, she heard not only the message but also the coughing of Reet and Nyakota's remaining daughter, three-year-old Nyakwic. This child clearly had whooping cough.

Nyakwic was in danger not only from the disease but also from local superstition. Someone in her village would try to convince her mother to cut under Nyakwic's ribs to release the evil in her body. If her mother refused, then others in the village would try to undertake the surgery themselves—or they would bring the Nuer medicine man to cut the girl.

Trouble compounded for Reet and Nyakota. Two weeks later, Nyakota's uncle died.

A family member approached Reet and Nyakota with a reprimand: "Reet! You have not placed your bracelet on your wife's uncle's grave. You must come now."

"I will not."

"You must."

"I will not."

"You will die!"

"No, I won't."

"You will."

"*Awhn* [Yes]. Someday I will die. But I am not afraid of taboos."

"Reet. Please."

"No."

Reet's brother came to see him, to save his life. He said, "Reet, I will go to the man's grave in your place. You do not have to do it. Give me a bracelet. I will do it."

"No."

"Reet . . ."

"No, my brother. I will not."

"Then, do not come near my house. Do not come near my children."

"You may always come here."

"I will not."

The testing of Reet's resolve strengthened his faith. Reet's and Nyakota's faith rippled out to the faith of the small band of Nasirite Christians—and Nyakota's feet became even more beautiful.

Nyakwic's coughing gradually subsided. The vaccine arrived. And, thankfully, the epidemic passed.

The Sunday before Christmas 1956, Kuac preached. He was the first fully ordained Sudanese pastor of the Nasir church. After church, Reet and Nyakota invited the local Christians to their home for a meal. They had finished a new barn, and they wanted to dedicate it. Arlene and Vandy went. The meal was served inside the barn. Reet had built a special fire pit at its center, as smoldering charcoal helped keep the mosquitos away.

The building itself was a testimony. Its grass roof was held up by long poles, and on the inside of the barn, the poles were plastered over with mud. On the mud, written in white chalk, were the words: "*Dwehl Reet Nyakota. Kwothdan e jen Jeethuth* [The house of Reet and Nyakota. Their God is Jesus]."

Before the meal, the assembly sang a hymn, and Gac Rik led them in prayer. Then Reet made a little speech. He said that the neighbors would say he was acting like some big chief inviting a group of people to his barn. "There is a chief we are celebrating," he said. "We are here in honor of our chief who is Jesus. This is his birthday."

Everyone sat on mats on the barn floor. Nya Top and Man Gac helped Nyakota prepare the food on little fires out in the *kaal*. The food was brought into the barn on one large platter and in many gourds. There was *kissara*, a large, thin dura pancake that could be torn, folded, and used to pick up other food. There was *mulaa*, spicy stew made with chicken, tomatoes, onions, and red peppers. There was *kuan*, an oatmeal-like porridge also made from dura. The food was eaten without utensils, and everything was shared in common. With glad hearts, the small band of believers broke off pieces of *kissara*, passed the gourds, and dipped their fingers into the feast.

 *13*

Jɔk Jak

Thurs. Thrilled with Elijah reading. Visited in Pts.
before brkf. Census takers here. Lesson with C.P.
Sewed trunk cover and moved it to my room. To
see Basheer's wife who thinks she is aborting. Very
nice prayer meeting—just Marian and me.

August 16, 1956

Dr. Gordon was gone for two months of vacation, leaving Arlene as the sole medical professional at Nasir. On a Thursday morning in the rainy season, she began her day as usual: reading from the Scriptures. Today's reading was about Elijah, the fire-from-heaven prophet who stretched himself on a dead boy pleading, "Lord, my God, let this boy's life return." Soon, he brought the boy to his mother, saying, "Look, your son is alive!"

After her morning prayers, Arlene crossed to the clinic *tukls* to check on her patients. She ended at Cieng Piŋ's *tukl*, where she took her morning language lesson. Then she had to get home. The new Sudanese government census bureau had come to town, and everyone was ordered to wait in their houses to speak with the census takers. There would be no clinic today. It was a good day to get some home projects done. After breakfast, Arlene did some sewing. She cut some of the leftover material from the pink bedspread she had made and had enough to cover her footlocker. She carefully quilted a top, even though she had never tried quilting before. For the sides, she sewed a gathered skirt of unbleached muslin and attached it to the top. She lowered the whole covering over the trunk at the foot of her bed. She was a Dutch-American farm girl, and her Nasir bedroom looked like her Midwest culture.

That same morning, forty miles away, a seven-year-old Nuer boy was walking in the family *kaal*. He was perfectly used to being among cows, so he knew to watch out for the horns. But then suddenly something terrible happened. Which cow did the deed? Later, anyone in the boy's family, including the boy himself, could tell you the cow's name. Not that the cow was to blame for what happened. Neither was the boy. It simply happened. A longhorn cow flicked its head, perhaps to shake off flies. The pointed end of a horn sliced the boy's abdomen, his intestines tumbled out, and he shouted as he fell into the dung.

The boy's mother, sitting in her outdoor kitchen, did what any mother anywhere in the world would do when hearing that particular cry of a child. She called out his name: "Jɔk Jak?" (*Jɔk* rhymes with hawk. *Jak* rhymes with rock.) Then she repeated it with more urgency: "Jɔk Jak!"

She was already on the run. When she got to her son, lying in the mud and dung, she could immediately see he was badly hurt. She did several things at the same time, as a mother can. She moved the cow. She calmed her son with cooing sounds: "Jɔka-Jɔka-Jɔka-Jɔka-Jɔka . . ." She picked her son off the ground. She then called for her husband, who came running.

Jɔk Jak's mother carried him inside her *tukl* where they could assess the wound. Clearly, two things would need to be done: the organs that had come out of Jɔk Jak's body would need to be put back where they belonged, and the boy would need to be taken to the "place of magic" where a more permanent solution could be found.

Nuer homes usually contained a few versatile tools. There were cooking pots, gourds, and spoons. There were spears, a hoe, and fishhooks. A fishhook would come in handy to sew up the boy's wound, but the family had no fishing line. The father ran to a cow and grabbed hold of its long tail, cutting off a few sturdy hairs with his teeth. He dashed back to his wife's *tukl* and took the fishhook from her trembling hand. He threaded the hook. Jɔk Jak's mother held back the skin while the father gently pushed the intestines under the flap of skin and then pulled the skin together. He pinched the skin and pushed the hook through the two layers, pulling the cow's hair tight. And again. And again. Jɔk Jak clenched his teeth together and tried not to move. Jɔk Jak knew he would need to be ready a few years from now when the cutter laid him down and sliced the six *gaars* across his forehead to show everyone he was a man. Jɔk Jak wanted to be prepared for that day, able to hold still—not flinch or cry out. Today was practice. Jɔk Jak did not completely succeed, but he did his very best.

When the final stitch was tied off, Jɔk Jak's mother and father gathered a few cloths to cover themselves when the rain grew coldest, and they headed toward the river. Laying Jɔk Jak in the bottom of a borrowed dugout canoe, the father paddled out into the deepest water. Although it was still midday, they knew they would have to paddle through the night.

Back in Nasir, Arlene spoke with the census takers, and then she walked across town to check on an Arab woman who was afraid she was having a miscarriage. Arlene told the woman's husband, Basheer, to keep his wife lying down and not allow her up to cook or clean.

The day ended quietly. There was no evening clinic. The generator was not powered up. Dusk fell, and in the lamplight, Marian and Arlene spoke their prayers together, back and forth at length, in sweet communion with each other and their God. As they lay down to rest on the screened-in veranda, they could hear the hippos splashing in the river and making their deep-throated grunts.

Twenty miles upriver, the prevalent sound was the rhythmic rise and fall of a paddle held in the strong hands of Jɔk Jak's father. Jɔk Jak's mother sat in the bow, peering into the dark for crocodiles and floating logs that might capsize the small vessel. Jɔk Jak lay in the bottom of the canoe, trying to hold still because every move hurt. Infection had already begun its work.

Friday morning began without a *luth ruun*, and dry weather meant there definitely would be a clinic today. Arlene looked out the window and saw dozens of patients already gathered under the great tree. Even so, she followed her normal practice of devotions followed by *tukl* patients. She refused to set aside her language lessons, ever aware of the longer-term goal. On this day, she would be particularly glad later that she took time for breakfast. Finally, she stepped into the clinic yard. One of her first patients was a man with a fractured bone in his finger. Although Arlene did not yet have access to an X-ray machine or the surgical skills of Dr. Gordon, she was able to diagnose a primary fracture using the "Does this hurt?" method. She set the bone as straight as she could, applied a splint, and wrapped it tightly to control swelling. One down—and a hundred to go.

After the clinic patients, Arlene crossed town to make a house call on Basheer's wife. The pregnancy was viable, thank God. She breathed a sigh of relief and returned to the clinic to give Nathaniel, one of the dressers, a lesson about asthma. When a commotion emerged at the riverbank, Nathaniel went to investigate and then came running back. "Nya BiGoaa!" he called to Arlene. "There is a hurt boy!"

Jɔk Jak's parents followed on Nathaniel's heels, carrying the boy, laying him at Arlene's feet. They would have collapsed from weariness and hunger, but their concern kept them desperately alert. Arlene saw the blood and pus on the boy's abdomen. She read the telltale symptom of sweat, and sure enough, when she touched his skin, he was on fire. She urged them all to gently move him to a table inside. Once there, she gestured, "Stay here" as she grabbed Nathaniel's elbow, ushering him into the lab.

Nathaniel had no idea what was expected of him. "What must I do?"

Arlene had brought him aside for a brief but simple purpose: "Let's pray."

They did pray in earnest. Returning to Jok Jak on the table, Arlene smiled down at him. He smiled back—a sign of hope. She took his temperature: 102. She applied a local anesthetic and then began an exploration. She severed the makeshift sutures and could see that the intestines were immediately below the skin. Arlene gently lifted and turned them to see if they were damaged. Other than having spent a day situated in a new place in the boy's body, they were miraculously unscathed. She gently pushed them back through the fat layer, abdominal muscle, and peritoneum, back where they belonged. She smiled at Jok Jak and he smiled back.

Arlene was not a surgeon, but she had been glad to assist surgeons during her days back at Methodist Hospital in Sioux City. She thanked God for having had those opportunities to watch and learn. On this day, she had no choice but to be the surgeon and her surgical team was the village dresser and the patient's parents. Normally, only necessary people would be in an operating room—Arlene knew about the importance of a sterile field. She also knew that if she chased the parents away, they would take their son with them.

Arlene swabbed the wound and installed a drainage tube for the expected ongoing infection, which was perhaps the boy's greatest enemy. She inserted penicillin powder directly into the wound. Finally, she repeated the parents' stitching, but this time with a sterilized needle and surgical thread, working her way outward through the various severed layers. Whenever the hovering adults smiled down at the young patient, he made an effort to smile back. He didn't make a sound, finally drifting off to sleep.

Arlene decided to fix him a bed there in the clinic, but she sent his parents out to a clinic *tukl* to get some rest. When she moved the boy from the surgery table to the clinic bed, he awoke. When she told him he had been a brave boy, Jɔk Jak replied, "My father is a very, very brave man."

That night, as Jɔk Jak lay where she could hear him call, Arlene wrote in her journal, *Please save him, Father.*

The next morning, Arlene brought her thermometer to Jɔk Jak's bedside. She was experienced enough to read the signs even before she read the numbers on the thermometer. His body was cool. The infection was under control. He would live. Arlene was thrilled to bring the boy to his mother and father: "*Gweeche! Gatdu tike* [Look! Your child is well]!"

Jɔk Jak had many days of recuperation ahead, but he had survived with a story to tell of his midnight canoe ride to the place of magic—and of the smiling nurse who told him he was brave.

The next morning, the man with the fractured finger returned. He needed his wound reexamined because it had hurt in the night, and he had removed the bandage. Nya BiGoaa reapplied the dressing, all the while giving him a *ruac mi bum e tet!*—a good talking to.

 *14*

Yuɔl

> *Sun. Tired and headache all day. Put cast on woman with fractured femur. Van & I good time over Joshua 3&4 in P.M. Waters of Jordan around us. Took stand against the devil. Kɔŋ & Yuɔl two clinic patients really saved.*
>
> *December 9, 1956*

"Something awful and gruesome at the clinic every day," is the way Vandy put it. But what the non-medical missionary might consider awful and gruesome was Arlene's raison d'être. On the other hand, Vandy's work—Nuer linguistics—was Arlene's "awful and gruesome." After months and months, she wrote in her journal, *Dreadfully discouraged about language. These tones and vowels seem impossible.* Difficult as it was, however, learning Nuer had to remain one of Arlene's highest priorities. This priority was not only practical for treating patients, but it was also mission policy. If Arlene did not make annual progress, the mission board might remove her. Therefore, she spent hours each day with Cieng Piŋ.

Finally, both Arlene and Cieng Piŋ took a break. Arlene left Nasir for a vacation, and Cieng Piŋ's healing from his tuberculosis allowed him to travel home for a visit. He had enough medicine to last the month, and he would return to his clinic *tukl* before the rainy season got underway.

Arlene's vacation took her from the rural south to Sudanese cities in the north: Khartoum and Port Sudan. Her life for a month was boats, trains, hotels, waiters, and a diversity of travelers—all wearing clothes. Food, clean water, and toilet paper were in plentiful supply, and electricity was available twenty-four hours a day. Arlene wrote home that her respite in "civilization" made her realize what an appeal "things" still had to her, and it made her disgusted with herself.

While Arlene was journeying, so was Cieng Piŋ, but his trip was by foot and canoe. He hitched rides on canoes upriver to the Pibor junction and then south to Akǫbo. After that, it was seven days of walking. He found friendly hosts, who allotted him a space in a barn or next to a smoldering fire in a *kaal*. Foxes have holes, birds have nests, and the traveling Nuer has the kindness of fellow tribesmen. He drank swamp water and dined on whatever his hosts offered. He walked in the way of the people and was at peace.

At his home village, Cieng Piŋ heard the cough of one of his uncles, an elderly man named Yuɔl (pronounced "You-ALL") Bithow. Based on Yuɔl's bloody sputum, Cieng Piŋ deduced that something was seriously wrong. It is not known whether Cieng Piŋ immediately shared some of his isoniazid medicine. Regardless, the supply was short. Both men required more attention, although Yuɔl's condition was clearly more desperate. Yuɔl had never been to the "place of magic" on the Sobat. Indeed, he would never make such a trip without someone to testify of healing and show the way. After some discussion with Yuɔl's two wives, the men started toward Nasir.

Vandy had entrusted to Cieng Piŋ some pages of her translation of the Gospel of John. Yuɔl could not read, so Cieng Piŋ read the story aloud as they walked, or as they sat under a tree to escape the heat of the midday sun, or as they borrowed rides northward in friendly canoes.

That Cieng Piŋ and Yuɔl made it back to Nasir alive is a tribute to tribal care. The two men followed the same path and depended on the same hospitalities Cieng Piŋ had used on his way home. The tribal markings on their foreheads were their identity cards for one more meal, one more night in a barn, and one more ride in a canoe. Although the journey was slow and took many days, at last they arrived at the clinic in Nasir and Cieng Piŋ introduced his uncle to his friend, Arlene.

Since the clinic X-ray machine was broken, Arlene's diagnosis could not be much more certain than Cieng Piŋ's suspicion. She took her young friend aside and said, "You know what's wrong with your uncle, don't you, my brother?"

"I thought so."

"You remember that I thought it might kill you?"

"Yes."

"You are younger and stronger than he is."

"I know. Still, I told Yuɔl that he should go with me to the clinic tree on the Sobat River at Nasir. He is come."

As the rains began to fall, Arlene cared for the old man. Yuɔl, though ignorant of the world outside of his southern *kaal*, was curious and talkative. He always wore a happy smile. If Cieng Piŋ had been Arlene's favorite patient, Yuɔl would soon claim the position.

Cieng Piŋ had Arlene practice her Nuer with Yuɔl by telling him the story of the Good Samaritan. When she was finished, Yuɔl said, "This talk is very sweet, my daughter." Yuɔl began to appear at clinic prayer times under the great tree. He attended Vandy's weekly Bible studies, sitting on the log bench in the grass-roofed church. He could often be seen on his little mat in the open sun, wearing nothing but two metal bracelets on his right wrist, two beaded necklaces around his neck, and a faded white cloth knotted at the left shoulder, draped over half his body. He was usually talking with Cieng Piŋ or Kɔŋ, a man who had been a big chief during the time of British rule. Anyone listening in would have heard them speaking of God.

Yuɔl would exclaim, "How many cows have I killed for the gods? One, two, three, four, five!" He counted on his fingers. Starting with his thumb, he bent each finger toward his palm until nothing was left but a fist. Each finger represented a cow whose name, colors, and offspring he could recite. "And did I get life? No. No life. They are gods of uselessness." He clicked his tongue several times to further assert the truth of the matter.

As he worked out his theology, he applied himself with great effort. He spoke to Vandy one day, calling her by her Nuer name, "Nyarial, do you know what God wants of us? He wants us to be his praisers!"

Yuɔl was drinking fresh water, and the more he drank, the greater his desire for more. Another day, he said, "Nyarial, I said to that man Ruon, I said, come let us talk. He came. I said you are an old man; let us talk about the God *Jeebuth*. Ruon says, I don't want to talk about the God *Jeebuth*. I said then go away. I don't have any other talk."

Like every other Nuer, Yuɔl did not say "s" sounds, but for some reason he always said *Jeebuth* instead of the usual "*Jeethuth*." Since Arlene and Vandy knew whom Yuɔl meant, they did not act like grammar school teachers over the matter.

Vandy was a lover of words and a lover of the Bible. Yuɔl's priorities and passions were helping Vandy refine her own priorities as a linguist. Oral culture can seem sloppy to a jot-and-tittle culture, but another perspective may find oral culture nuanced, flexible, and understanding rather than legalistic. The culture Vandy discovered in the Sudan exploded her theories of Bible translating and, she ultimately would claim, precluded the possibility of producing an "exact" or "inerrant" translation of the Scriptures.

Throughout the rainy season and then into the dry heat of December, Yuɔl conversed and considered the Christian way. Although he did not fully know what it would cost him to walk from Nuer animism into the way of the cross, he finally decided to step in. One cannot know for sure, but one factor may have been the ancient river story that Vandy and Arlene had discussed with Yuɔl one Sunday. It was the story of the miraculous parting of the Jordan River as described in Joshua 3. The river flowed until the priests carrying the Ark of the Covenant stepped into the water. Then the river piled up, and the Israelites walked across on dry ground. With the Sobat River flowing by just steps away, Yuɔl bowed his head and said, "*Jeebuth*, you are now my God. I will have no other." Arlene wrote in her journal that night: *Waters of Jordan around us. Took stand against the devil. Kɔŋ and Yuɔl two clinic patients really saved.*

In the days that followed, the weather suddenly changed and a north wind began to blow. By early January, the temperature had dropped to 54 degrees, which was unusually cold for southern Sudan. Yuɔl's enthusiasm for his newfound faith was contagious. Day by day, there were more visitors at prayer meetings. The third Sunday in January, there were twenty testimonies given during worship.

Yuɔl announced, "I want to be washed." He meant, of course, that he wanted to be baptized. He had never seen a baptism, but he had heard the story of John the Baptizer and the River Jordan. So on the last Sunday in January 1957, there were eighteen baptisms, including Yuɔl, his friend Kɔŋ, and Arlene's friend Nya Top.

With two months to go before the rainy season, Yuɔl spoke with his caretaker: "Is it peace, my daughter?"

"It is peace, old grandfather," Arlene answered.

"Nya BiGoaa Jon."

"Yes, old grandfather."

"It is still the season for travel. Am I well enough to go home?"

"No. You still need to take the medicine every day."

"You can give me the medicine to take to my home."

"You are safer here, old grandfather."

"I will be with my family there. I wish to see my people. I wish to talk to them."

Vandy joined the conversation, because she was concerned for Yuɔl's young and vulnerable Christian faith.

"You are safer here, old grandfather," Vandy said. "There is danger if you go. Much danger. You should stay with us."

Yuɔl placed a finger on his own chest. "There are many hearts in my village. God is churning for the hearts of my village. I wish to speak to them of *Jeebuth*."

Vandy and Arlene had themselves journeyed far for the cause of Christ. How could they tell this man that the Great Commission did not apply to him?

Vandy said, "It is good talk."

Arlene said, "Go in peace, old grandfather."

Yuɔl said, "Stay in peace, my daughters."

The day he left Nasir, Yuɔl prayed, "God of the sky, Father of *Jeebuth*, protect me from the father of evil when I get home. You know the temptations and power of the way of the People. Oh, protect me. *Inono* [Amen]."

As he sailed away from Nasir, hitching a ride in a dugout canoe, Yuɔl shouted back to his friends, "He is my husband! God is my husband!"

Vandy said, "He seems to have no question of the love of God for him."

Arlene replied, "He is so happy."

After his canoe had disappeared downriver, Vandy admitted to a fear. She was afraid that Yuɔl was about to enter a perilous phase of his spiritual journey; she wondered if his conversion would last. She had encountered grim demographics concerning some Christian converts who had first been part of another religion. "Consider Buddhists, for example," Vandy told Arlene, "They tend to return to Buddhism at the time of their death. They may live a Christian, but they die a Buddhist."

"What are you saying, Vandy?"

"BiGoaa, I have as much hope as you. But we have to face the fact that there are many dangers in the Christian way."

"I'm a Calvinist. I believe that if he is a Christian, he will remain a Christian."

Vandy gave a simple but loaded response: "If."

The rainy season finally began, and Cieng Piŋ moved to Khartoum to resume his education.

A Nuer man from Yuɔl's area came to Nasir and gave a report on Yuɔl. He said that the old man was continuing in the Christian way. Yuɔl had devised a method of seven sticks to help him know which day the Christians at the clinic would be worshiping. On the day of the seventh stick, he celebrated a Sabbath for his God who he declared was *Jeebuth*. Someone placed a shrine to another god in Yuɔl's *kaal*. Yuɔl took the shrine down, but all is not at peace, said the man.

The rainy season progressed, but Yuɔl did not return to Nasir. Arlene knew that Yuɔl did not have enough medicine to last beyond the rainy season. He must return.

Cieng Piŋ wrote to Arlene from his school. It was a troubling letter.

> *My sister, I have heard bad news that my uncle has sacrificed a cow to the gods. He is an old man, but a babe in Christ. I think of Yuɔl as a Daniel in a den of lions. We must not forget to pray for him.*

The believers at Nasir prayed, but Yuɔl did not return. The hot and dry season came back, but Yuɔl did not. Then in mid-December, the Nuer man from Yuɔl's area returned with a dire message: "He won't live long. He can never reach Kuanylualthoaan by foot again. The disease of before has come again. His son died. The family said, 'It is your fault, Yuɔl. Make a sacrifice to the god *Deng*. Live or at least let us live.' So the animal was killed. And Yuɔl is still dying."

Vandy angrily proclaimed that the devil was not going to beguile this lone sheep of the Lord's without some opposition. The next day—Tuesday, December 17—Arlene, Vandy, and Reet caught the Missionary Aviation Fellowship (MAF) plane to Akobo. The women did not know what their next step would be. It was a journey of faith. The MAF leg of the trip was the easiest and took only one hour.

Wednesday dawned bright and beautiful. Verne, the mechanic who had repaired their boat two years earlier, prayed them on their way at 6:30 a.m. They set out in a borrowed Willys Jeep, loaded with food, water, bedrolls, and extra gasoline. They drove on the government highway—a one-lane dirt road. Traveling sixty miles in three hours, they arrived at Cieng Piŋ's home village of Waat. Yuɔl's daughter told them that her father could be found at the cattle camp further out in the bush. A boy knew the way to the cattle camp, but he told them, "There is a problem. You cannot get there by car."

Arlene said, "If we don't take the Jeep, we can't get him out. He'll die."

Vandy said, "Get in the Jeep."

"You cannot take the Jeep," repeated the boy.

"Would you like to ride or walk beside us?" Vandy asked him.

The boy said, "I will take a ride."

They started out in the desperate heat of midday, across the trackless plain, through the tall grass, creeping over the hummocks of caked earth left on the floor of the dried swamps. A family of giraffes loped gracefully alongside them. There were suddenly small marshes filled with large, white water lilies.

And then the hood of the Jeep bounced off.

They tied it back on with a rope and continued the crawling, jolting ride. The Jeep overheated, so every twenty minutes they stopped to refill the radiator. On one of those stops, they noticed that a battery cap had wiggled its way loose and was now gone. Reet whittled a stopper from a root, and on they went.

There were no villages to mark the way, but the boy saw something and said, "Go there," pointing with his tongue as the Nuer do.

The others looked, but there was no "there" there.

The boy said, "Go to the tree."

Way in the distance stood a small tree, like a black mast on a calm sea of golden grass. The Jeep sailed up and down toward the tree, but there was no one there.

The boy again pointed his tongue toward the far horizon. "Go. Go there."

Vandy said, "There's nothing there! Nothing at all!" But it was a journey of faith, so they pushed forward. Finally, the boy said, "He is here."

At first, they saw nothing. Then, looking carefully, they saw one more tree in the distance—short, thin, and lifeless against the gray sky. The Jeep crept closer until the horizon dipped, revealing a small waterhole filled with men and cattle. And then they saw him. Yuɔl was coming to meet them, leaning on a staff, draped with the new white cloth the mission had given him. Arlene and Vandy got out of the Jeep and ran.

Vandy said, "Sit, old Grandfather. Come and sit down. Is it peace? Is it peace?"

"My children. I am dying. I am dying."

The boy went to bathe in the water hole. The others sat under the small tree, with Yuɔl in its narrow shadow.

"I did something. I killed an ox. There has been much trouble. My son died. I am dying. The father of evil came to me."

He may have been thinking of the devil, but more likely he was referring to his first wife. She did not accept his Christian beliefs, and Yuɔl would sometimes say that he slept with the father of evil.

"My head was confused," he continued. "Everyone was angry. They said God was angry, and it is my fault—that is why we are dying. But *Jeebuth* loves me, this I know."

The threesome sat at the foot of the tree and spoke together of the goodness of Jesus. They sang, "*Ken kocke, ka Jen bume* [They are weak but he is strong]."

Arlene laid one of her large hands on Yuɔl's forehead. "We have come to take you back with us, old Grandfather."

Yuɔl smiled and shook his head. "The journey will kill me."

"But there is a sky canoe that is coming to take us all tomorrow."

"A sky canoe?" Yuɔl put his hands on either side of his head and was silent. Then he said, "*Wane* [Let's go]."

After she helped Yuɔl into the Jeep, Vandy pulled Arlene aside. "Just for the record, I'll be surprised if the trip in this Jeep doesn't kill him."

For once, Arlene agreed with Vandy's half-empty glass, but they had no time to lose if they were going to reach the road before dark.

The boy stayed at the water hole, and Yuɔl sat in the back with Reet holding him in the seat, attempting to cushion the blows of the jolting ride.

At last, they saw a lone merchant shop, indicating the government road. They stopped for supplies. Vandy overheard two Arab men talking about them, the men not knowing that she was a linguist who understood their every word.

"Who are those two white women?"

"They came to get the old man in the Jeep."

"Who is he?"

"He's that old man from Pi Jiaak. Yuɔl. The man who has Jesus for his God."

Vandy suddenly started laughing, and when Arlene asked her why she was laughing, Vandy whispered, "Because he hasn't lost his faith. Even the Muslims know what he believes. If they know, everyone must know."

The next day, Betty Greene flew them back to Nasir on the only airplane ride of Yuɔl's life. He sat on the floor of the "sky canoe," refusing to look out the window, saying over and over, "What is God doing! What is God doing!" He was not himself until his feet touched the dry grass of the Nasir airstrip.

Although Yuɔl improved some, he developed a blood clot in his leg and became very weak. Clearly, death was near. This was the moment of Vandy's greatest concern. She would later write:

> For anyone professing Christianity [the] attitude at death or in the face of death was the big test. [If that person] affirmed allegiance to Jesus, or negatively, did not succumb in fear and resort to calling on a heathen god, it was noteworthy.

Yuɔl turned out to be noteworthy. His last request was to avoid any superstitious funeral practices. "Do not bury me in the way of the people," he insisted. "Cover me only with the white cloth. Nothing else."

Vandy assured him, "Yes, old Father, you will be buried in the white cloth as you have said."

At the end, an old woman who knew Yuɔl sat near him, smoking a pipe with a long stem.

Vandy came into the clinic *tukl* early in the morning.

The old woman asked her, "He will die today?"

"I don't know. Maybe. His body has nothing more. Did Yuɔl talk to you of God?"

"*Awhn.*"

"Did he tell you about the place he is going?"

"*Awhn.* He said he was going to the place where God is."

"Which God?"

"The God *Jeebuth.*"

"The God *Jeebuth*?"

The woman took a drag on her pipe. "The God *Jeebuth.*"

Vandy asked the old woman, "Do you believe this is true?"

"I don't know." Suddenly she stared at Yuɔl. "He died?" She wanted to be ready to turn her back, because that is what the Nuer do when death comes.

Vandy said, "No. He is breathing still. The place of God is a good place, old mother. Maybe there are cattle there."

"It is like that?"

"It may be. God said he was getting it ready for us."

Vandy was familiar with this promise and had translated Jesus' words about the place of God, as reported in the Gospel of John. Vandy did not know if there would be cattle in heaven, but she believed that anything in heaven would be good—and she knew that for a Nuer, nothing was as good as cattle.

The woman suddenly said, "He dies." Then she spit and turned her back.

Although none of them—Vandy, Arlene, Reet, or Kuac—could know with certainty, they believed Yuɔl had crossed the Jordan with his faith intact, calling back to those on the shore, "*Awhn! Jeebuth nhok a* [Yes! Jesus loves me]."

They ferried Yuɔl's body to the bamboo grove where he was lowered into the grave as he requested, emptied of all his jewelry, and covered only with the white cloth. After the earth was pushed on top of Yuɔl, Kuac read from the Gospel of John, "The hut of my Father has many places. If this were not so, I would have told you. I am going to make ready a place for you. When I get the place ready for you, I will come back. I will take you as my people."

Before Arlene turned in for the night on January 27, 1958, she wrote a letter to her folks in Iowa. The letter was in ballpoint pen, which is unusual as she typed most of her letters. There was something else unusual about the letter—there are places where the ink has run, as if drops of water splashed onto the page as she wrote:

> *There can be no greater contrast than someone moving from a Nuer hut into a heavenly mansion. It was exactly one year ago today that he was baptized. I remember his joy that day and he said to me after the service, "Ci lɔcda teth e yiam"—"My heart is full of happiness." He was a dear old man and probably one of the greatest joys of this term will have been to know him.*

15

Spending the Day in Heaven

Have thought so much about the Mystery of God's Will. Amazed that He wants to share His secrets with me. "I will give thee the treasures of darkness, and hidden riches of secret places. . . ." Isaiah 45:3

September 30, 1959

Arlene's favorite picture of Pa is one of the first photos she took with her Argos C3, back when it was a brand-new camera, a gift in anticipation of her move to Africa. She was standing out at the road along the south edge of the farm. Pa posed in the farmyard, facing the camera, hands on his hips. In the photo, he's in his winter gear—hat, gloves, medium-length coat, overalls tucked into his boots. His cattle and pigs are in the feedlot in front him. Many of the cows seem curious about Arlene's activity, and they have turned their white faces toward the camera. The snowfall is so fresh that the Herefords' reddish-brown backs seem dusted in powdered sugar. The pigs are all snoot-down, but their busy rooting has not yet created any mud. The yard is white. The barns behind Pa are perfectly red, trimmed white at their doors, windows, edges, and eaves. The house is white. The treetops are white. With Jack Frost's assistance, the photo has a striking, limited palette of red, brown, and white.

That picture was snapped the same month Arlene left the farm, on her way to an ever-humid home by a wandering river in the flat-as-a-pancake southern Sudan. Four years flew by, and now she was back in America for her first furlough.

Things had changed at the farm. Pa was no longer working the feedlot, and Ma was no longer making her daily climb down to the potato cellar. Arlene's home place was now in the care of her sister Bernice and Bernice's husband, Howard.

It was the custom in the Midwest to keep farms in the family. One child would be selected as successor to keep the business going. Weddings were scheduled to facilitate efficient transitions. March 1 was known far and wide as "moving day." One generation moved out in the morning. The next generation moved in after lunch. In one day, the Schuiteman home had become the Sandbulte home. Throughout Arlene's life, however, she and her sisters would continue to refer to the place simply as "the farm."

On the last day of February 1959 at 1:30 a.m., Arlene disembarked from the plane in Sioux City, Iowa. Pa and Ma were there to fetch her, eager to have their number two daughter home, and eager to show off the brick bungalow they had built on 2nd Avenue two years earlier. Arlene's sister, Grada, was living with them. Milly was off at college, but in the summers, she and Grada shared the small house's extra bedroom. Arlene's quarters would be in the basement, which was just fine with her.

Arlene was home only for a few weeks before the folks bundled her into the car for the all-day drive to visit her sisters, Milly and Joyce in Holland, Michigan. Milly was attending Hope College, and Joyce's husband, Wilmer, was preparing for the pastorate at Western Theological Seminary. After their visit, Arlene and her folks, along with Aunt Delia, squeezed into the back of her Uncle Gerrit's green Ford and headed south. After an especially long day's drive, they arrived at their destination in the mountains of southeastern Kentucky—Hyden, an isolated county seat with some three hundred town-dwellers. The bulk of the county's residents lived in the surrounding Cumberland Mountains, connected by dirt roads, creek beds, horse paths, and foot trails.

What attracted Arlene to Hyden was the Frontier Nursing Service. Founded in 1925, FNS sought to reduce that region's high infant mortality rates. In 1939, the service started its own graduate school to train midwives.

During her four years in Africa, Arlene had developed a passion to combat infant mortality. Further training was needful, and Arlene especially appreciated the Frontier Nursing Service's emphasis on rural and underserved populations. For over a year, Arlene had been looking forward to spending half of her furlough at the Frontier Graduate School of Midwifery.

It was dark when Arlene and the folks wound their way into the little town. Arlene was assigned a room at Marti Cottage, which housed the seven students of that year's class. With no motel, it looked as if the folks might have to sleep in the car or drive back into the night, until they discovered there were beds available in the maternity ward. Aunt Delia, who had not been able to conceive children of her own, laughed over the idea that she would finally get to sleep in a maternity bed.

The next morning, Arlene was up at six o'clock to say goodbye to her aunt and uncle and Ma and Pa. She would not know until months later just how significant this parting was.

Arlene and her six classmates plunged enthusiastically into midwife boot camp. After morning lectures, the students attended to pre- and postnatal patients who were capable of traveling into Hyden. Next were duties in the hospital maternity ward and swinging shifts between days and nights. Every sliver of free time, if one could call it that, was filled with studying for the final exams looming at the end of six months.

The list of midwifery duties was far from complete. Since many patients could not travel to Hyden, the midwives had to travel to the patients. Frosty and Junko were the names given to the World War II army surplus Jeeps that carried the intrepid midwives uphill and down, through creeks and over brush-filled paths, until the nurse had to get out and climb the rest of the way to cabins hidden in the hilltops and hollers. When the Frontier Nursing Service started in 1925, there were no roads. Jeeps were now the future, but the service maintained their horse tradition as well. The nurse's traveling uniform was a white shirt with a long blue vest and matching blue jodhpurs stuffed into tall riding boots. Each midwife carried specially outfitted saddlebags, whether she was making a call on horseback or by Jeep.

One Sunday morning, Arlene and her fellow student, Margo, rose early to clean the horse stalls and pitch manure. One of them remarked, "We're in graduate school!" The disconnect between expectation and reality sent them into giggling fits. The rest of the day was church, letter writing, and then, for two of the midwives, an all-night supervision of a face-presentation delivery near Wolf Creek. With no Sabbath in between, Monday's clinics started the workweek all over again.

Each student would have to go on calls. The goal was a minimum of twenty deliveries by each midwifery student during her final months in Kentucky. Each of the midwives in training hoped for a phone call or a knock on the door with a man's voice saying, "My wife's a-hurtin.'" And off they would go.

The roads were treacherous and took time. Travel was often in the dark, through unincorporated townships with names such as "Hell For Certain." The nurses were concerned with the possibility of BBA (Birth Before Arrival), so they always rushed. Once Arlene was called to Red Bird, and after parking the Jeep at the end of a road, she had to make a steep twenty-minute climb on foot, lugging her saddlebag. She began to wonder if this delivery was going to be a DNA (Dead Nurse upon Arrival).

The cabins were often constructed of rough-cut lumber, covered with unpainted vertical, overlapping siding. After just a couple years, such a building became encased in brush, with the brambles and tree branches threatening to reclaim the cabin's wood as their own. Dogs, cats, a pig, or a cow ran free in the yard or, if the animal was small enough, rested in the cool shade under the open-sided porch. The railing of the open veranda was useful as a clothesline. To many Americans, these mountain homes would be considered inadequate—but to Arlene, these properties seemed like mansions compared to a *kaal* in Nuerland. She thought it a privilege to be invited inside them. Once, when she assisted at a particularly hard labor, a chicken roosting in a cardboard box at the side of the bed laid an egg and began cackling just as the baby was born. Arlene laughed and laughed.

The mountain folk were kind and, whenever possible, generous. They made a sleeping place for Arlene during protracted labors. They always offered plenty of food, although she had to discern what to accept. She learned by experience that her stomach might not be adequately prepared to accommodate the local bacteria.

Having inherited her Pa's penchant to do everything early, Arlene completed her required twenty deliveries well before school was over. As she entered her final week of midwifery school, Arlene was not feeling well at all. She wondered if the cause was dysentery, flu, or perhaps even malaria. The possibility of sickness concerned her, since Tuesday would be final oral exams and Thursday the written State Board exams. Then she needed to pack before Pa, Ma, and Grada picked her up for the long drive back to Sioux Center. This was not the week to get sick. On the first day of the week, she wrote in her journal, *Somehow this was an odd day—as if I wasn't being directed by Him—I don't like days like this.* She dropped into bed early with aching bones.

On Monday, she was up at six, feeling a little better. At 3:30 in the afternoon, a phone call came for Arlene Schuiteman at the hospital switchboard. The call was transferred to Marti Cottage.

"Arlene?" a woman asked on the other side of the receiver.

Arlene immediately recognized her voice. "Grada! Hi."

"Arlene . . . it's Pa," Grada said.

"What?"

"We're in the hospital."

"What is it?"

"He and Ma were going with Joyce and Wilmer to Sioux City to pick out a piano. They only got a mile outside of town when he started feeling bad. Wilmer wanted to bring him straight to the hospital, but he thought he'd rather go home."

"Oh, no."

"He was in his chair. And he got to feeling worse. So they drove him over here. And called me at the Co-op."

"What are they saying?"

"Coronary thrombosis."

"Oh, my."

"Yeah."

"Can he talk?"

"Not right now. I'll have him call you. I'll tell him."

Arlene hung up, grabbed her Bible and diary, and left the cottage. She followed the path up the hill, past the old mine, to her prayer rock—a large flat stone big enough to completely sprawl on, which is what she did. Arlene was in the habit of citing in her journals biblical passages she read as well as prayer lists. They formed a road map of her interior life. Today she wrote the names of all her family members. She did not forget to mention those she had left behind in Nuerland. She prayed through supper. Shortly after she returned to the cottage, another call came for her.

It wasn't Pa . . . because Pa was gone.

Arlene's classmates kicked into action. Peggy reserved flights. Molly started packing. Barb brought everyone into her room for prayers. Marg read favorite Bible verses as they spoke the references.

Arlene's flight would be Wednesday, so tomorrow, Tuesday, would be her last full day at the Frontier Graduate School of

Midwifery. She would have to complete all her departure arrangements, finish her oral exams, and take her written exams early. She couldn't sleep, but she was too sick and tired and numb to study. Her exams would have to reflect what she already knew. No further preparations were possible. If this cessation meant that the last six months were in vain, so be it.

In Sioux Center, Pa's body was embalmed and prepared for return to the house on 2nd Avenue. In this era, visitation happened in the family home. Plans were made for Ma and the girls to meet Arlene at the airport in Sioux City prior to the visitation.

Arlene took all her exams and said her goodbyes to these women who had, in six short months, forged friendships that would last the rest of their lives. Weary and weepy, she headed off to catch her flight. There was bad weather that caused delays, and when she finally landed in Chicago, her flight to Sioux City had already departed. She raced to a pay phone and caught Ma and the girls just as they were leaving to pick her up. Now the goal was to get home by Thursday, the day of the funeral. Visitation would begin Wednesday night, so Ma and the girls would need to be home. They could not pick up Arlene.

Two houses to the north lived Pete and Gladys, favorite cousins in the Schuiteman clan. By the time Arlene had arranged to fly into Omaha, Pete and Gladys were ready to pick her up wherever and whenever she arrived. They delivered Arlene to 2nd Avenue at two in the morning on Thursday, the day of the funeral. When she entered the house, she noticed that the folding partition between the dining room and the living room was closed. Knowing what was in there, Arlene chose to leave it closed that night.

Early in the morning, she crept up from the basement room and slid open the partition to the living room. As she expected, there was the bodily temple her Pa had lived in while on earth. Arlene crossed the room and opened the front drapes. Strangely, large flakes of snow began to fall as the sun rose. Arlene had her Bible in her hand. She knew where to open it today. She read the same passage Kuac had read in the bamboo grove over the body of Yuɔl:

> *Don't let your heart worry. You believe God, so believe me also. The hut of my Father has many places.*

Arlene wrote in her journal, *Oh, Jesus come quickly.*

Later that morning, Grandma Schuiteman arrived in her black dress, carrying the purse that every child in the family knew contained pink and white peppermints for sharing. The octogenarian stood over her son's body. "My child, my child," she moaned in Dutch. "My baby in your cradle."

Soon it was time to go to the church. The undertakers closed the coffin and gently carried it out the front door. Ma commented on Pa's foresight. His friend and lawyer, Maurie Te Paske, had told him when they built this house, "Make sure the doorways are wide enough for a coffin." Pa had followed Maurie's advice, but no one expected his good counsel would be needed so soon.

As the family moved up the steps to the sanctuary, Mr. Riphagen, the custodian, tolled the bell in that special way, inviting anyone within a half-mile to stop and pay respects.

Later that night in the now-strange house, Ma and her daughters sang a hymn. Singing with others had been a godsend to Arlene all her born days.

Arlene received a cablegram from Marian back in Nasir. The spelling was mangled by the operator—Arlene was *ORDENE* and

Marian Farquhar was *MAREANE FORGUAN*—but Arlene understood. She knew that the simple, tan half-sheet represented many
prayers. The cablegram read:

ALL THANKS OF YOU LOVING YOU REJOICING
WITH YOU HIS SUSTAINING POWER
JON THIRTEEN ONE.

Rejoicing? At a time of such tragedy? Yes, because this trial was also
known by their leader, Jesus. Marian rejoiced because she believed
that the love and care Jesus had extended to his twelve disciples
was now being extended to Arlene as well. As it says in John 13:1,
"Having loved his own which were in the world, he loved them unto
the end."

Vandy sent one of her usual breezy airform letters, full of news,
church politics, good humor, and faith. She was never one to be
stopped in her tracks by death. Her Lord had not been stopped by
death, and she intended to follow his footsteps no matter what or
where. Nearing the end of the letter, she transitioned effortlessly
into comforting her friend:

> *There is no doubt but the Lord knows what He's doing. He has*
> *brought to you and to your whole family very deep pain. The*
> *deeper it goes, that's how deep He must go to bring comfort,*
> *and the deeper God goes in a life the more precious He becomes.*
> *I can even feel the pain right now out here. As tho it happened*
> *to me. And it hurts. This continues to be preparation for more*
> *that is ahead in order to strengthen the "legs" of faith that they*
> *will be able to stand when the blast hits.*

On November 4, word came that the midwifery students of
1959 had all earned As on their exams, including the one who wrote

her exam two days early because her father had died suddenly of a heart attack.

At the end of December 1959, Arlene sent a brief letter to her supporting churches and friends, summarizing her furlough year and expressing her desire to be back at work among the Nuer. The final paragraph tells of Pa.

> *How grateful I am that I was in this country at the time. And so there is something very special about this Christmas. This is the first Christmas that we have someone from our own family spending the day in Heaven with Jesus, our Savior and Risen Lord! We worship Him as He removes the sadness and fills our hearts with His Joy.*

> *With Christian love,*
> *Arlene*

16

The Fly

*Fri. A blanket of new snow as we awaken to
a New Year. What will this year bring? May
it lead me to a fuller, deeper knowledge of
Him. He was faithful in 1959 although I never
knew more difficult times. My anchor holds
and grips the solid Rock. That Rock is Jesus.*

January 1, 1960

Arlene knew she was back at her African home when she saw the smoke from the cow-dung fires wafting across the Sobat.

Cow-dung fires heated Nuer meals and created the ash that served as a body rub to keep away mosquitos. That same ash served as a base for makeup and hair colorant on days of marriage dances. A cow's excrement was not perceived as dangerous in any way to the Nuer. A Nuer man might even wash his hands in a cow's urine stream as part of his morning toiletry. A Nuer woman might place her mouth against a cow's vagina and blow to encourage the cow to release its milk into its udder. The Nuer mother of a newborn child would have a bit of cow's manure placed in her mouth before she took her first postpartum drink of water. And if a Nuer person was experiencing diarrhea, a recommended tribal remedy was to combine tobacco and steer urine, boil it down to a paste, and insert it into the rectum.

Arlene was at war with disease and therefore opposed to certain aspects of Nuer culture. Perception of dung as dangerous was a new idea to the Nuer, and it was even a relatively new idea within modern medicine. A hundred years earlier, nursing pioneer Florence

Nightingale published her *Notes on Nursing*. She argued in support of the commonly held position that the "first and last thing upon which a nurse's attention must be fixed" was the air a patient breathed. She and her medical colleagues did not understand that bacteria were more likely to spread through what a patient ate, drank, and touched. Medical professionals of Nightingale's era did not bother to wash their hands when moving from patient to patient. If Florence Nightingale had been serving in the Sudan, she would have been more concerned about the cow-dung smoke than the fact that cow dung and human waste washed into the river where Nuer women dipped their gourds for drinking water for their children.

One of the greatest enemies in the fight against disease among the Nuer was a creature that appreciated cow dung even more than the Nuer did: the fly. Flies rushed to the latest cow dropping. You hardly saw the flies coming, but suddenly a cow pie was covered with them. After the insects soaked their feet in manure, they landed their soiled feet on people. Most Nuer moved about with nothing but beads and a smile, so flies were landing directly on their skin all day—which they just ignored. Just as people who grow up in the rural Midwest learn to ignore farm smells that waft across their countryside, the Nuer hardly noticed the flies they brought with them wherever they went.

Flies were carried to the clinic tree on clinic days. Flies were carried into the clinic. Clinic days were disease transference days. It could hardly be helped.

The dry season was the busiest time of year for the clinic. During the dry season, the Nuer moved toward the river and set up cattle camps across from Nasir. Medical conditions that had been put off until cattle camp days could finally be addressed. The clinic crowds were higher starting in November and grew until the rainy season began in April. Some days there were as many as six hundred and fifty patients—all of whom were cared for by one doctor, one nurse, and a few Nuer dressers.

Here's how a clinic day worked. Arlene arose when it was still dark. She did her morning prayers and Bible reading. She dressed in her white nurse's uniform, slipped on her white shoes, and stepped outside. By sunrise, the crowds were already gathering.

The patients sat under the large sycamore tree that served as a signpost as well as protection from the sun. The dressers moved a table under the tree, and Arlene brought out the box of five-by-seven-inch index cards. On each card a patient's name was written. If a patient had visited the clinic previously, that person's medical history would be recorded on the card. If the patient had not been at the clinic, a new card was started. Once a patient's card had been placed on that day's stack of cards, the patient was asked to sit and wait.

The physician sat at the table with the cards of the patients who were present. Patients crowded close and began muttering "*Hakim* [doctor]" and scratching the *hakim* on the elbow or running a finger down the doctor's arm. The doctor ignored all the muttering and finger poking and called the name on the top card. The named patient squeezed up to the table. The doctor conducted an interview, examined the patient, and wrote a recommendation on the card. The doctor then put the card onto another stack and asked the patient to wait a bit longer. After a while, one of the dressers would invite the patient to follow him into the clinic to receive medication or treatment. Through this system, hundreds of patients could be helped in a matter of a few hours—while thousands of flies accompanied them.

At 9:00 a.m., a rest period was called, when Dr. Gordon, Arlene, and the dressers took time for breakfast. The patients breakfasted before leaving home, purchased bread from local merchants, or fasted. The Nuer were used to two meals a day, and during lean times, they became good at fasting. During the morning rest period, one of the clinic staff usually prayed with the gathered patients and told a story from the Bible, a practice that served both as evangelism and much-appreciated entertainment. After half an hour or so, clinic rounds resumed until all the patients had been seen. Then Dr. Gordon and Arlene moved inside for lab work and surgeries.

The most common surgeries were for eye conditions. Dr. Gordon had a special concern for an eye condition brought about by the disease of trachoma, which was spread by the pervasive flies. The flies started their insidious work by teaching the Nuer to ignore fly feet on their bodies. A Nuer would learn at a young age to let flies walk all over their face, including eyelids and eyelashes. The moisture there provided a fine laboratory for growing trachoma bacteria. The flies then carried the bacteria from person to person. About half of the children experienced recurring trachoma.

If Dr. Gordon determined that a patient had trachoma, then the first step was to control the infection. The eyes were washed and treated with ointment. Patients were given one tube of ointment and asked to continue treatments for seven days and then return to the clinic.

Trachoma was a disease that, if untreated over a long period, created a condition called "trichiasis." Trichiasis was a buildup of scar tissue that tipped the eyelash forward. Eventually eyelashes would start to brush over the eyeball, scarring the cornea. If left untreated, trichiasis would lead to blindness. Flies led to trachoma that led to trichiasis that led to blindness. Dr. Gordon set out to stop the process.

Trichiasis could be treated with a simple surgery. A bit of skin of the eyelid above the lash was removed, and the two surfaces were sutured together. The eyelashes were suddenly back where they belonged, and the cornea would once again be protected and not scraped. The surgical area was covered with ointment and sterile gauze, protecting the eyelid while it healed in its reclaimed orientation. The entire procedure took Dr. Gordon and Arlene about fifteen minutes. The patient would need to be led home by a family member and then brought back a week later for the stitches to be removed.

Dr. Gordon and Arlene began doing trichiasis surgeries in April of 1956. The first of their patients soon had clear eyes and a story to tell. For each patient they treated, however, three new patients arrived. Before long, trichiasis surgeries were up to about ten a day. Arlene wrote in her journal: *More eye operations—Father, show us how to manage.*

Arlene was not alone. Her family and home church were always looking for ways to help. Allie Scheffer, a friend from the First Reformed Mission Band, began knitting eye bandages according to Arlene's specifications.

Arlene noticed that trichiasis surgery was done most often on unmarried young women. Her hypothesis was that when the time came for marriage negotiations, a girl with inverted eyelashes was not worth as many cows. When a father learned that there was a procedure at the "place of magic" that could make his daughter more valuable, he brought her to clinic. It cost him a dollar per eye, but who knows how many more cows it brought to his *kaal*.

Besides morning clinics, there were evening clinics with "only" a hundred or so patients. And then there were emergencies, which were treated day and night.

As if she didn't have enough to do, in 1961 Arlene received a visit from Pastor Kuac on behalf of the church elders, asking Arlene to start health and cleanliness classes for the women of the church. Arlene agreed, and Kuac translated Arlene's lectures into Nuer. Vandy typed them, using a typewriter specially outfitted with the Nuer alphabet, and booklets were printed in Malakal. Not every woman could read, but the girls attending Marian's school could carry the booklets home and read them to their mothers.

Here is an excerpt from Arlene's lecture on clean drinking water:

> *Why do so many small children die of dysentery in this country? I will tell you. Maybe one person has dysentery. He passes many stools in one day. Some of them he passes along the riverbank. When the rain comes, it carries the stools down into the river. A woman goes to the river to get water. She*

fills her pot. She does not know that the germs are in her pot because the germs are too small to see them.

The woman's baby is crying when she reaches home. She gives the baby a drink of the water from her pot. The germs from the water go into the baby's stomach. Many babies die in this way in this country.

What can you do? You can boil the water. A man would die if you place him in boiling water. Is it not true if something as large as a man will die in boiling water, then very small things will die if you boil the water?

You must boil the river water before you drink it. You will always put the cover back on the pot to keep the flies out. You will have one very clean bottle with a cover. You will put the water for the baby in it. No other person will touch it. A strong person may have power to fight a disease. A small baby has no power.

You will never pass a stool near the river. If there is no latrine, a person could carry his hoe and cover the stool so that the rain will not carry it to the river and the flies will not sit on the stool.

No, you must not say that it is too much trouble. How long did you have your child in you before it was born? Is it good to carry a child in your body for nine months and then let it die of dysentery because it is too much trouble to boil the water? A person will think very much about this. She will not say it is too much trouble. God will help that woman.

Arlene's lectures on hygiene were intended to guard the health of Nuer women and their families. On August 24, 1961, a storm grounded the plane of Sudan's military ruler, keeping him in Nasir overnight. While he was in town, the district commissioner toured him around, including a stop at Arlene's hygiene lecture. Little did Arlene know that her good intentions would one day provide the justification for her expulsion from the Sudan.

17

The Boy Who Fell

Dear Ones:
This is Sunday and probably the saddest day that we
as a mission family here in the South Sudan have
experienced for as long as I've been here on the field.

The beginning of Arlene's letter
home (April 23, 1961)

At the height of the dry season of 1961, the morning clinics became overwhelming—over five hundred patients a day sat under the clinic tree hoping for attention. Dr. Gordon and Arlene could not keep up. Patients who needed trichiasis surgeries were told to come back another day. And then another. Soon there was a long backlog.

On the first Thursday in March, a truck arrived at the Nasir mission station. One of the people on that truck was Lowrie Anderson, the general secretary of the Presbyterian mission in the Sudan. It was Lowrie's first observation of the Nasir clinic during this time of year. On Friday, he stood at a distance and watched the crowds waiting in the shade of the clinic tree. There were five hundred and ten patients that day. Although Lowrie was impressed with what was being accomplished by one doctor and one nurse, he was concerned. He returned to observe the clinic on Saturday morning when there were even more patients than the day before. As Lowrie watched, a woman became hysterical, creating panic in the large crowd. The woman was restrained by the police, and Lowrie went to speak with the district commissioner. The DC's observation was, "They should have another doctor."

"They would have one if you would allow another one into the country!"

"No, you must get a doctor who's already here."

"Then the government of the Sudan should do that."

"It's not our clinic. It's your clinic."

"Then let us provide a doctor!"

"You should provide a doctor from one of your other clinics."

"No, those clinics need their doctors."

"Do they need them as much as this clinic?"

Lowrie knew that the answer was no. There was no clinic in as desperate a shape as Nasir.

That evening, Lowrie called for a meeting of station personnel, which Dr. Gordon, Arlene, Vandy, and Marian attended.

Lowrie spoke with supportive urgency. "How many patients come to the clinic each day?"

"Over five hundred."

"Every day?"

"Five days a week. We take Thursdays and Sundays off."

"Well, I don't see how you can continue like this."

"In two months, the rains will come. Then we'll be back down to three hundred a day."

"Two months is too long to keep up this pace. You're one doctor and one nurse. Marian and Eleanor, you have your own tasks. It simply shouldn't be expected. It's not right. I'm your supervisor. It's wrong of me to let this go on."

"What do you suggest?"

"You could take another day off. Maybe no clinic on Tuesdays?"

"Then we'll have eight hundred patients on the remaining days."

"All right. We'll close down the Pibor clinic for a week at a time and bring the Roodes up here. Their kids are all off at school, and Pibor can miss them for a week. Would that help?"

Dr. Gordon and Arlene nodded.

"And, Arlene, I want you to stop teaching the women's health classes."

Vandy groaned.

Lowrie responded, "She's not superhuman."

Vandy spoke up, "I know, I know, but the reason these people come to the clinic in hordes is because they don't understand the most basic . . ." She stopped herself.

"Go ahead, Vandy."

"Nothing. I know we're all at the end of our ropes. Something has to be done."

Lowrie said, "I'll talk to the Roodes. And I'll get you the money to hire a few more Nuers for crowd control."

Vandy quipped, "So you don't need me anymore for crowd control? What'll I do instead? Oh, Bible translation. I almost forgot."

Lowrie left Nasir immediately after church the next morning. True to his word, on Wednesday, the MAF plane landed on the baked earth with Dr. Al Roode and his wife, Ruth, who would serve as surgeon's assistant. This was good timing because that week's clinics grew to six hundred and fifty patients a day.

Dr. Roode and Ruth were a bit older than the missionaries already at Nasir. Back when he was just a teenager, Al Roode had read about the medical mission to the Sudanese people. His heart had been captured, and he nurtured his longing until it became a reality. In 1946, Al and Ruth began their work in the Sudan at Doleib Hill. In 1952, the Roodes founded Pibor Post, the most isolated of the American Presbyterian mission stations. There were only brush and trees on the riverbank at Pibor when the Roodes motorboated there with their three young sons. The news of their arrival spread quickly, and on their second day, Dr. Roode met patients outside his family's tent. Ruth assisted her husband as needed, learning medicine on the job. Now, nearly a decade later, the Roode clinic was well established in service to the Merle tribe.

Up in Nasir, where the Roodes came to help, there were typically no clinics on Thursdays. Now, since the Roodes were here and ready to work, they all decided to make hay while the sun shone.

The clinic doors opened, the word spread, and soon the ground under the great tree was covered with sick people.

The Nasir medical team was able to treat more patients, but Arlene's fatigue was not immediately assuaged. Instead, it grew worse. The Roodes helped them catch up with surgeries, but the clinic had even more patients and the hours were growing longer. Arlene was hardly ever a complainer, even in the private space of her journal, but during the first few days of the Roodes' helpful presence, she wrote in various entries: *oh so tired, beginning to feel exhausted, feel exhausted, very weary,* and *just bushed.*

To complicate matters, it was the month of Ramadan and the Muslim population of Nasir fasted during the daytime. The Ramadan faithful were not permitted to drink water or even to knowingly swallow their own saliva. The lack of hydration in this blistering time of year may have contributed to an exceptional amount of illness in the Arab community. Arlene, however, suspected that this increase of "illness" was because the Muslims were permitted to drink water if they needed it to take medication.

A special Ramadan drum was pounded every day at 2:00 a.m. to tell the faithful to get up and eat before sunrise. The drum happened to be near Arlene's bedroom. After awakening to the drum, she dozed until 5:15 when her alarm got her up for morning prayer.

Scheduled to stay only a week, the Roodes stayed nine days. They worked hard, and the surgery waiting list was impressively diminished. Arlene's spirits rose.

The morning after the Roodes departed, when Arlene began removing stitches from the first surgeries Dr. Roode had completed, she made a terrible discovery: there was something wrong in his process, and the trichiasis surgeries had not been successful. When the stitches were removed, the surfaces had not healed together—they released, allowing the eye lashes to once again brush against the cornea. On Tuesday, Arlene removed more stitches. These surgeries also failed to hold. She could not tell if the problem had been in the sterilizing process or in the surgeries themselves. The sterilization process was Arlene's responsibility. The surgeries belonged to the Roodes. Whatever the cause, almost none of the surgeries succeeded in permanently changing the angle of the eyelashes.

That night, Arlene was so tired she could not fall asleep. She lay awake thinking of Pa. She remembered how he would always come to her when he had splinters.

"Arlene, I got one for you."

When she touched the needle to his finger, he would always howl in pain.

She would say, "Oh, Pa," and he would laugh.

She longed for those days of simple problems and simple solutions. She wished she could remove a sliver for Pa just one more time.

Two weeks later, the day after Easter Sunday, the Roodes returned for another go at the surgical waiting list. Dr. Gordon took Dr. Roode aside and explained that there had been a problem with the surgeries. The two doctors agreed on a plan, and the work resumed.

During those days, a dust storm called a *haboob* (Arabic for "blasting") blew through, followed by a *luth ruun* (heavy rain). The blasting wind covered the yard, walks, and trees in fine dust. Then the heavy rain turned the dust to mud. The mud hung on the electric lines, and soon the lights went out, just as they would in an ice storm back in Iowa. Since there were no electricians to call, the two doctors traded their scalpels for screwdrivers.

The day of the *haboob* and *luth ruun* was not the only wet weather that week, and due to the difficulty of travel through the water and mud, the clinic crowds soon dwindled to three hundred a day. The medical staff began to catch its breath. The countryside donned a fresh green robe. Al and Ruth finished the entire backlog of trichiasis operations.

There was a special clinic on Sunday, April 16, prior to morning worship. The trichiasis patients were examined. They were healing properly! Just before noon, the Roodes climbed in with Tony, the MAF pilot, and the plane lifted off the wet grass. The Roodes had completed one hundred and forty operations in ten days.

Arlene had grown in affection for Dr. Roode and Ruth. They had shared many meals and prayer times over the two short terms the Roodes had spent at Nasir. They had been lifesavers, and now they were family. Arlene had learned about Al and Ruth's four children: one of them was in college in the States, and the other three were at a boarding school in Egypt. The school term was almost over, and the kids would be headed home in a few weeks. The whole Roode family anticipated their upcoming reunion, especially since they hadn't been together since August the prior year.

The following Wednesday, when a cataract patient missed his appointment, Arlene used the extra time in her schedule to write a letter to the Roodes. It was the only letter she would write that week.

Seven days after the Roodes left Nasir, the radiotelephone (RT) crackled to life as it did every morning. This was a scheduled RT call, and someone at each station was on hand to write down the day's messages. Today, Lowrie was calling from Malakal, and he had a special request. He asked that everyone be gathered at the radiotelephones. Runners went out, and in minutes, station members at Doleib Hill, Ler, Akobo, Nasir, and Pibor were standing by. They knew there must be big news.

"Are the Roodes there?" said Lowrie.

Ruth keyed the mic from Pibor, "He's not here this morning, Lowrie. I'm here. Al's gone with the DC and some government guys down south to Boma."

"When will he be back?"

Someone joked, "This is Africa, Lowrie. Who knows?"

Ruth said, "In a couple of days, I suppose."

"Can the Swarts hear me?" asked Lowrie.

Morrie Swart, another of those at Pibor Post, said, "Yes," but added that her husband was not there.

Lowrie asked where he was. He was stalling now.

"Bob's somewhere between Malakal and Akobo," said Morrie. "He'll probably make it home tonight."

Someone keyed the RT and asked, "What's up, Lowrie?" Then there was a long silence.

"I've got news. Terrible news." Pause. "Ruth?"

"I'm here."

"Your son Joe's been killed." More silence. Lowrie said, "He was—." He couldn't say any more. A colleague, Robb, fumbled with the RT mic and told the story—but he eventually broke down too.

Joe was the Roodes' second child, and he was known as a good boy. At sixteen years of age, he was almost a man. He had lived in America, Egypt, and various places in the Sudan, but Pibor Post was home. He loved Pibor, and his heart had caught fire for translating the Scriptures into the language of his Merle friends.

Along with all the school-aged children of the various mission families of the region, Joe was in a boarding school in Alexandria, Egypt. The Schutz American School was an excellent private school where the classes were taught in English. Joe was in his last year there, his brother Philip was in eighth grade, and their little sister was in sixth grade.

The school was housed in a gated compound in an urban environment. Alexandria is a coastal city, so the school was only blocks from the Mediterranean Sea, and breezes off the water blew across the campus. The Schutz American School was not a Christian institution, but all of Alexandria could not help but know its history as the city in which St. Mark, the evangelist and author of the Second

Gospel, founded a church and was eventually martyred for his faith. The city is a world-famous holy center of one of the oldest continuing Christian groups, the Coptic (meaning "Egyptian") Orthodox Church.

One of the outings the school liked to take was a half-hour drive down the coast, followed by a left-hand turn and a short drive into the desert. As one drove, out in the middle of the sand, one could suddenly see the tall spires and cathedral dome of the St. Mena Monastery. The monastery and its surrounds have been a pilgrimage destination since the third century, and outside the cathedral grounds are the archeological remains of the city of Abu Mena. Under those ruins are tunnels and catacombs, waterways and cisterns. In 1961, long before the location was designated a World Heritage Site, those ruins were playgrounds for goats and local children. It was perfectly acceptable for tourists and school field trips to explore the ancient site unimpeded.

On Friday, April 21, the Boy Scout troop based at the Schutz American School left for the ruins at Abu Mena. They camped in the desert overnight, learning to light fires and cook outdoors. The night air was cool, and it was a grand adventure. Joe Roode was one of the older boys. Given his level of maturity, he was designated as a Junior Assistant Scout Master.

After breaking camp Saturday morning, the Scouts were encouraged to explore. Joe was eager to teach the younger Scouts respect for the carved stones and any artifacts they might unearth. Joe had great affection for archaeology, especially a site that was connected to the ancient story of his Christian faith.

There was, however, one rule Joe intended to break. He planned to climb down into the deepest cistern.

Joe was keenly aware that this was his final trip. A couple of months after school was out, his family would be heading to America on furlough. When Joe's two younger siblings and his parents returned to Pibor Post, Joe would not be with them. He would stay in the States for college. It might be years before he was back in

Africa at all, and he might never again return to Abu Mena. From Joe's perspective, today was his last opportunity.

One cistern had always been off-limits because of its depth. Joe was curious, and he apparently had the idea that few persons, if any, had stood on the bottom of the large dry cistern. There might be artifacts there that had fallen in and gone unnoticed for centuries. Whether or not he found any relics down there, Joe had a secret goal of reaching the bottom of the deep cistern before he left the school.

Joe was growing in wisdom and stature, but he was, after all, a boy, and on that April Saturday, he did a boyish thing. Out of sight of the two adult leaders, he enlisted his younger brother and two other Scouts to secure the upper end of his rope, and he began the descent into ninety feet of darkness.

Why did he stop halfway down? No one knew, nor would anyone ever know. For some reason, he stopped and then tried to pull himself back up out of the dark. He could not, so he called to the boys at the top that he needed their help. Joe's brother Philip strained at the rope. Another Scout helped Philip while a third Scout ran. In a matter of seconds, their leader, Mr. Small, was at their side. Others arrived. The only way to help Joe was to pull him up. They pulled, and Joe held on.

Then the rope went slack. The weight was simply gone. Did Joe's strength give out? Did the rope grow slippery? Did Joe lose consciousness? Was there lack of oxygen? Was there a deadly gas? The answers are unknown. What is known is that they did not achieve their goal—and a boy fell.

Those gathered at the top of the cistern heard Joe moan. He was alive. Mr. Small took a risk and climbed down the rope, calling Joe's name. When he reached the bottom, he checked Joe's pulse, but his Junior Assistant Scout Master was gone.

Mr. Small created a sling, and the others pulled up the body. Mr. Small took most of the boys back to town, while another leader and two Scouts stayed until the police arrived. A doctor examined the body and said that Joe could not have suffered long.

In 1961, communication was difficult at best. Bodies were not embalmed. Due to the desert heat, burials needed to take place very quickly. It was perhaps unusual to wait even until the next morning. The funeral service was set for 8:00 a.m. on Sunday. Joe's brother, sister, schoolmates, and teachers were present. His mother learned the news as his body was put into the ground on the Lord's Day.

Tony, the MAF pilot, set out that Sunday morning on a terrible errand: to find a father and tell him a parent's worst nightmare. This way, at least father and mother could comfort each other and their other children.

Tony flew south, keeping his eyes on the dirt highway from Pibor to Boma. Finally, in the distance, he spotted the dust being kicked up by the government convoy. There was no place to land, so Tony cut his Cessna across the path of the lead vehicle to get their attention. They probably thought it was a friendly wave, but Tony circled back around and flew directly toward the vehicles. Tony wrote a note that said something along the following lines:

> *There is sad news about Joe. It came over RT this morning. He was accidently killed in Egypt yesterday. If you want to return to Pibor by truck, then show that by turning around. Otherwise drive on to Boma, and the plane will fly you home.*

He tied the note to one of the large clods of dirt he kept rattling on the floor of the plane for just such a purpose. When the plane was in front of the vehicles on the ground, the dirt clod message sailed out the window. The convoy stopped. Someone got out and found the dirt clod. Then the vehicles on the ground drove on. Tony pulled back on the stick and headed into Boma.

Shortly after sundown, the convoy arrived at Boma. Then the missionaries at every station within range heard Al's voice over the radiotelephones, "Boma, calling Pibor Post." Then they heard Ruth Roode's voice answer, "This is Pibor Post."

At earliest light, Tony flew Al home.

Many of Arlene's Nuer friends would say, without cynicism, that Joe did something wrong and was punished for it. They might warn that the gods were demanding a sacrifice from Joe's family—if the sacrifice was not given, then someone else in the Roode family would die. The ancient religion of the Nuer people, like many religions all over the world, has to do with balancing the scales of justice and somehow appeasing a god.

The missionaries listening at the radiotelephones that day— Lowrie, Robb, Tony, the Roodes, the Gordons, Marian, Vandy, and Arlene—did not attempt to accommodate the scales of justice. They accepted the coexistence of despair and hope. They acknowledged their own aching hearts. They believed there would be a time to dance but also a time to mourn.

That everyone is born and everyone dies.

That there is a rainy season and a dry season.

That some grain may be eaten and some must be planted.

That some things must be stitched up and some must be cut out.

That some things should be loved and some should be hated.

That there is a time to flee and a time to wait, a time to speak and a time for silence, a time for work and a time for rest.

Arlene's own perfectionism wearied her. She was learning that there was a time for struggle and a time for letting go. Today she affirmed that if she—or Joe—let go, they would not fall into oblivion, but into the arms of a loving God.

There is one final piece of the story of the boy who fell. A week or so following the tragedy, a letter arrived at Pibor from Alexandria. It was Joe's last letter to his parents, mailed before his scouting trip. He spoke of his love for the Sudan, for its woods, its animals, its culture, and its people. He said that leaving the Sudan would be sort of like dying. Then he signed his letter with the sweetest words a parent can receive: *Love, Joe.*

18

The Unscrupulous God

*The clinic might well be called "The Wild Place"
today. Giving and drawing blood . . . 3 children with
foreign bodies in ears or nose . . . man with deep
head wound . . . Muslim child for I.V. . . . etc., etc.*

May 22, 1961

*God whispers to us in our pleasures, speaks in
our conscience, but shouts in our pains: it is his
megaphone to rouse a deaf world.*

C. S. Lewis,
The Problem of Pain

"Ten, nine, eight, seven . . ."

Cape Canaveral, Florida, 9:34 a.m., Friday, May 5, 1961.

"Ignition. Liftoff. Ahhh, Roger. Liftoff."

The local time at Nasir was 4:34 p.m. when Alan Shepard rocketed off the launchpad to become the first American in space. Arlene headed over to the Gordons' for supper. After supper, Dr. Gordon and Arlene performed a cataract surgery. Before going to bed, Arlene wrote in her journal that the U.S. had sent a man into space. A strange light sailed across the Nuer sky, and some who saw it sacrificed a cow.

The world had tipped.

Change, whether for better or worse, will always be accompanied by surprise and grief. That is what happened to Omer Mohammed, a Nasirite Arab Muslim who became a Christian.

A few days after Shepard crouched in his capsule, *Freedom Seven*, Omer returned home for the rainy season break from his boarding school in Khartoum. For some reason, he came to the clinic. Omer had been raised in Nasir, and his family still lived here. His father was a merchant at the local *suk* (market).

Omer was a bright and curious seventeen-year-old and would be starting college soon. His life was becoming his own responsibility. He was asking serious questions, and he asked one of them out loud in perfectly clear English when he encountered Arlene and Marian on the clinic grounds: "Why are you here?"

"What do you mean?"

"Why are you people doing what you're doing?"

"What people?"

"You Americans."

"Doing what?"

"Taking care of people. I know the patients pay the doctor, but they pay only a coin. He could be a rich man in America, but he sits here under a sycamore tree. Why does he do that? Why do you do it? It's not for money."

It was a good question. Arlene could answer in several ways. She was here because her parents had taught her to love people. She was here because her Sunday school teachers had taught her the Bible. She was here because God had called her through the preaching of Dr. Harrison and Reverend De Jong. She was here because of a supernatural experience in her home church. She was here because her denomination had sent her. She was here because she loved nursing and the nursing needs were great here. She was here because Jesus has modeled a life of caring for people's bodies and their souls.

Arlene put all of that in a sentence. "We're here to tell people about Jesus."

Marian nodded.

"You're Christians?" Omer asked.

"Yes."

"You're People of the Book?"

"You mean the Bible?"

"My religion reveres the stories of Abraham and Jesus, but we do not read them. We believe they have been changed and can only be known through the Qur'an. I have not read the Bible, but I would like to see for myself."

"Would you like to see my Bible?"

"I'd like to see one in Arabic. Can you do that?"

Marian said she would get one.

A few days later, Omer invited the missionaries to the Islamic New Year's Day or *Hijrah*, the Arabic word for "flight." The day commemorates Muhammed's escape from persecution—his flight to Medina where he founded his theocracy.

Hijrah was a day with entertainment and food, and many people were present—Arabs, the Nuer, and Americans. Many of the Arab men gave speeches in Arabic that were then translated into Nuer. Arlene heard many urgent appeals to worship Islam's prophet as the one true God.

That afternoon Arlene met a Nuer woman on the path who asked her, "Is that God your God too?"

Arlene didn't feel it was the right moment to untangle the stories of Judaism, Christianity, and Islam, so she simply said that she followed the God *Jeethuth*. The woman seemed content.

That was Friday. On Saturday, Omer came to the mission. He heard Marian had something for him. She gave him his Bible in Arabic, and he asked her where he should start reading.

"Can you find the Gospel of John?"

"Where is it?"

"In the New Testament. The first four books are about the life of Jesus."

"I've heard about the four stories."

"The fourth one is called John. It starts, 'In the beginning.' That's the same phrase the whole Bible begins with: 'In the beginning.'

But this time, the beginning is about . . . well, read it for yourself. You'll see."

The missionaries at Nasir read from their Bibles every day. They read privately, and they read to the patients at the clinic who had neither Bibles nor the ability to read. In the evenings, they studied passages together. They truly were People of the Book.

Like the other missionaries, Arlene read from her Bible, but she also read other things. Medical journals. Magazines. Letters. Books. In 1961, she read eighteen books, making a growing list of them in the back of her journal. Her list that year included *The Four Loves* by C. S. Lewis, one of her favorite authors. Lewis could have warned Omer that his curiosity would get him into trouble. In Lewis's memoir of his own coming into Christian faith, *Surprised by Joy*, he reflected on his transition from atheism:

> I did not know what I was letting myself in for. A young man who wishes to remain a sound Atheist cannot be too careful of his reading. There are traps everywhere—"Bibles laid open, millions of surprises," as Herbert says, "fine nets and stratagems." God is, if I may say it, very unscrupulous.

Although Omer's Muslim family loved him very much, if they had found his Bible, they would have thrown it away. They were too close of a family to throw Omer away, but life would have become more difficult for them all. Omer was therefore careful to delay their knowledge of his growing faith as long as he could.

The next Monday, Omer returned to see Marian, carrying his Bible under his white *jalabiyyah* (robe). He had begun reading the

Gospel of John and had some questions about the first verses: Who was meant by "the Word"? Was that the same person as "the Light"? Was John saying that this person points to God the way a prophet points to God? Or was John saying that the Word was the same as God? Was the Word actually God?

Marian smiled. Yes, she said. Yes.

Omer asked Marian if she could show him how she prayed. She said that usually she closed her eyes and bowed her head. So they did. Marian thanked God for coming to earth as one person with many descriptions: the Truth, the Way, the Life, the Light, the Christ, the Messiah, the Word. She thanked God for providing a book of true stories. She asked God to continue to teach her and Omer about *Isa* (Jesus in Arabic). She said, "Amen." Omer said, "Amen." He tucked his Bible back inside his *jalabiyyah* and said he would return after he read some more.

After Marian had told Arlene about her conversation with Omer, Arlene wrote in her journal: *Could it be that the Lord has placed the new Life in him?* As C. S. Lewis wrote in *Mere Christianity*:

> And that is precisely what Christianity is about. This world is a great sculptor's shop. We are the statues and there is a rumour going round the shop that some of us are some day going to come to life.

The next day, Tuesday, Arlene conducted a blood transfusion with Bob's supervision. The cause of her patient's anemia was undetermined, but it was nevertheless acute. The woman's relatives said she had been listless for over a year. Over that year, they had sacrificed ten cows and two sheep, but none of it had helped. Only as a last resort did they bring the woman to the "place of magic." It was probably best that these people were desperate, since taking blood from family members to place into the woman would otherwise have been an unthinkable barbarism to them. Bob and Arlene, however, believed that a transfusion would give the woman new life.

At first, the woman's husband would not agree to the procedure because some of the blood was to be taken from men. He could not understand putting a man's blood into a woman's body. He loved his wife, however, so he accepted that this incredible act of mixing bloods might save her.

Transfusion was a new procedure to Arlene. On her furlough in 1959, she had collected the equipment for transfusions, but this was the first occasion that seemed to justify the necessary battle with cultural taboos.

The female patient lay flat on her back on the dirt floor of a clinic *tukl*. Her right arm was bound to a board. A bag of blood hung from the rafters above, with the clear plastic tube descending to the woman's arm. Many family members, some of whom had donated the blood, sat watching the blood flow into the woman's arm.

The ten cows and two sheep had been sacrificed to the gods Deng, Kulang, Bil, and others. Did this Nuer family ultimately come here for Arlene's medical skill or for the power of her God? Did they even make a separation between the nurse and her God?

Arlene had met Nuer who believed that if they could only touch her body they would be healed. She would tell them, "No, I'm a person just like you!" Arlene drew a clear distinction between humanity and divinity, between the physical and spiritual. When Arlene used the phrase "new life," she might have been referring to something temporal, but she also used the phrase "new Life" when referring to spiritual and eternal. How could she explain the distinction to these people who were watching blood drip down from the rafters? Now that she had convinced them that there was life in the blood, could she also get them to see that there was another Life even more substantial?

The woman got better, and Omer got "new Life." Both changes happened quickly.

Omer said simply, "I don't know how to explain it. But I can feel it inside."

His experience reminded Arlene of C. S. Lewis's experience as recorded in *Surprised by Joy*:

> I was driven to Whipsnade one sunny morning. When we set out I did not believe that Jesus Christ is the son of God, and when we reached the zoo I did . . . like when a man, after a long sleep, still lying motionless in bed, becomes aware that he is now awake.

Omer had only a few more weeks before he returned to school in Khartoum, so he read the Bible like crazy. He finished the Gospel of John and then asked Vandy what he should read next. She suggested John's letters as John was Vandy's passion. She knew that John the apostle had written his letters to new Christians just like Omer. John's Epistles were a primer for the Christian life.

The next weekend, Marian invited Omer to church, and he accepted. The Monday after that worship service, Omer sat on the veranda at the mission, discussing the book of Acts, when three Arab men suddenly stopped by. Omer slipped his Bible inside his robe, but they knew why he was there. They were indeed following him, watching him. After they left, Omer said that he was afraid the men would pressure his father to make Omer an outcast. The men did go straight to Omer's father but, thankfully, Omer's family did not cast him out. There were, however, quiet changes, like not touching things after Omer touched them. For some reason, they did not destroy his Bible.

The following weekend, the missionaries invited Omer to the station for Sunday dinner. Arlene made meatloaf, scalloped potatoes, squash, and fruit pie. The missionaries touched what Omer touched. That night, Vandy led the worship service. She asked Omer if he would share his testimony. He agreed. Arlene said later that it was the most thrilling thing.

During his final week in Nasir before returning to school, all Omer cared to talk about was the Bible and what he had just found in it. He didn't have any other talk.

One of last times Arlene spoke with Omer was on a visit she made to Khartoum. He told her that he was experiencing some persecution from his classmates as well as his family, but he was still making plans to be baptized. He said to Arlene, "It is necessary for a Christian to suffer if they are to understand the spiritual truths and grow in them."

You truly are a Christian, thought Arlene. You are taking up your cross.

19

With Painful Labor

Sunday. Khartoum. To Arabic service . . . then
spoke at Nuer service. Genesis 3. Felt the Lord
led. Student nurses went on strike and Ministry
dismissed them all! Omer visited, but I wasn't home.

November 12, 1961

On a Wednesday evening, Arlene was called to the home of a Nasir government official whose wife was in labor. Examining the woman preparing to deliver, Arlene immediately observed the effects of Female Genital Mutilation (FGM), which was called "female circumcision" at that time. This practice caused the author Michael Langley, in 1951, to dub the Sudan "the most disagreeable country in the world in which to be born a woman." Arlene had never seen such mutilation of a Nuer woman, but she had come to expect that every Arab mother she attended would be maimed like this government official's wife.

This mutilation was presumed to quench a woman's lust, guard her virginity, and increase her husband's enjoyment. In this woman's case, her clitoris and labia minora had been removed. Then her labia majora had been scraped to prepare the skin to be drawn tight and sewn shut, leaving a miniscule hole for secretions. The procedure was probably accomplished prior to puberty.

Although Arlene had no opportunity to ask this woman to share how she had gotten like this, especially given the labor contractions, she had heard stories of what this woman might have experienced as a child. Maybe, as a little girl, she caught a glimpse of her older sisters when they were naked and saw that their private areas were different from her own. When her mother took her to the Nasir clinic tree for medicine, she saw that her private areas were the same as the naked tribal girls who were there. Those girls had a crevice down the center of their girl parts, as she did. If they went over to the grass to relieve themselves, their private areas split apart, as hers did. But her sisters' never split apart like that. They had only a small hole, and their water came out in drops, not a stream like hers did.

When she asked her sisters why they were different down there, they said, "Your special day will come."

"What do you mean?"

"Don't worry about it. It's not your time."

"Will I grow up to be like you?"

"It will happen all at once."

"When?"

"When you're old enough."

"When?"

"Someday. Some morning. Don't even think about it now."

"What will happen on that morning?"

"You will become a woman."

She looked forward to her special day when she would become a woman.

Then one morning, before she turned nine, her mother whispered to her, "Tomorrow is your special day. I will make your favorite food for supper. But you should not drink much water today. Try to get as dry as you can today. Make yourself empty."

"Why, Mama?"

"Never mind now. Tomorrow you will see. But try not to drink."

She did not drink all day, and she got so dry she didn't have any sweat under her robe and her mouth got sticky. She didn't talk much.

It was hard for her to get to sleep, because tomorrow was going to be her special day. She awoke when her mother whispered, "It's time. Get dressed. Do not eat now. Follow me."

When she went outside, she saw her sisters, her mother, her grandmother, her mother's friend, and another woman she did not know. They were humming and collecting sticks and grass to make a little shade shelter. Her sisters were smiling at her and giggling at one another. She didn't ask any questions, because she had been told to wait so many times, and now she knew that her special day was here.

The other woman struck a stone on a piece of metal. She said nothing except "Lie down." Then the little girl's mother said, "It's time." Her sisters cooed and laughed. She laid herself down, and her mother knelt behind her and put her hands down heavily on her shoulders. Her mother said, "Shush now. Try not to cry. It will be over very soon."

Her sisters grabbed her ankles and tied pieces of cloth around them to hold them apart. Her grandmother prayed. The other woman stood between the little girl's legs, and the little girl instinctively closed her knees together. The other woman made a gesture to spread them, and the sisters each grabbed a knee and pulled. The other woman disappeared, her grandmother prayed louder, and her mother's friend began to sing. The little girl screamed.

Her mother had not told the whole truth. Only the first part was over very soon. The business with the piece of metal was over. Then the other woman said, "Give me a thorn." The little girl's grandmother came and looked things over. She nodded her head and made a happy clucking sound. Then the little girl's grandmother handed the other woman a thorn. The little girl felt piercing pain. Again and again. She heard her mother's friend singing. Then her grandmother handed the other woman some pieces of string. There was a lot of fussing and saying, "Hold this end. Tighter." They pulled the string and then tied it. The process seemed to last forever.

Finally, the other woman stood up. The little girl's grandmother clapped her hands. The sisters stopped pulling the knees apart and untied the pieces of cloth from her ankles. They straightened out her legs and pushed her knees tight together. Then they wrapped the pieces of cloth around and around the little girl's thighs so they could not separate. Her mother lifted her onto her feet and then gave her a little push toward the shelter. The girl almost fell, but her mother supported her and told her to move her feet. The little girl found her balance and shuffled her feet. When she arrived at the shelter, her mother swept her up into her arms, bent down under the sticks, and laid her on the ground.

All the women started chattering about how well she had done. Her mother left her and handed something to the other woman. The other woman unfolded the bundle and counted the coins. She picked up her piece of metal, waved her hand, and went away.

The little girl's womenfolk sat by her and stroked her forehead. Her mother rubbed some water on her lips. Her legs were shaking now, but she couldn't stop them. She pressed her lips together and shut her eyes tight, trying to stop the moans coming from her throat. Her mother's friend hummed and her mother made a *shhhhhhh* sound—like a soft wind. Her oldest sister hovered over her face and blurted out, "Now you are a woman." Everyone except the one lying down laughed and whooped.

Arlene imagined the little girl living outdoors under the shelter for three weeks, rolling over to relieve herself with great pain. Her private part had a small hole, the breadth of the stem of a leaf, large enough to let water out a drop at time. Then came the infection and terrible pressure, the most dangerous part of the journey.

After she returned indoors, being a woman was an ongoing challenge. The infections never seemed to quite go away. Relieving herself was a challenge that required daily planning. Menstruation arrived as a monthly horror. However, she carried a particular pride—the knowledge that womanhood was difficult, and she was truly becoming a woman, like her sisters, and mother, and grandmother.

Then there came another special day. The little girl who had become a woman got married. On her wedding night, her husband examined his bride. He confirmed with a glance that she was a virgin. Now something had to happen for her to give herself to her husband. The other woman, or one like her, was asked to bring her piece of metal to the bridal chamber. She could not repair what was gone, but she could open a closed door. She did not open it very far. She checked her work with the width of two fingers. Then she and the husband went away, and there was a waiting period of three days, after which the marriage officially began.

Arlene noted that the contractions were one after the other. The room had filled with women: family, friends, and neighbors. The swell of each contraction was accompanied by the swell of joyful ululations. There was no man present, not even the husband. No male doctor would have been allowed: Arlene was in the embrace of an ancient sorority.

Arlene could now see the infant's head pressed against the inside of the vaginal scar tissue. The tissue would tear unless Arlene brought her own piece of metal to bear. She took her scissors from their sterile wrappings. She carefully but efficiently severed the tissue, upward and downward, performing a double episiotomy.

The baby slipped through just after midnight.

There was a collective intake of breath. Waiting. Silence. Then the baby's first cry filled the house, followed by an explosion of joy. She quickly wrapped a blanket around the infant to contain its heat. The father was soon in the doorway. Arlene held the baby toward him, saying, "You have a little girl!" Arlene knew what he would do, but she always hoped that the response might be different. He leaned toward the child, glanced at its face, nodded his head, and then shuffled out of the room. If the child had been a boy, the father would have taken the babe into his arms, and there would be no quieting the man. The sorority took over in the father's absence, cooing and taking their turns holding their newest affiliate.

The little girl had two older sisters waiting in the next room. Arlene could hear their giggling through the wall. Those older sisters were two and four. Arlene thought about them and their futures. They were probably not yet circumcised. Would the mother do the same that had been done for her? Once a woman has lived through this bloody tradition, would she actually put her daughters through it? Or would she put a stop to it?

This woman will not stop it, thought Arlene. This woman will reason that a little trouble in the present is better than terrible trouble later. To her, the terrible trouble is that a woman who is not "circumcised" will not be acceptable to marry since there will be no proof of her virginity. The terrible trouble is that she may develop sexual desires, just like foreigners. She will be called unclean. She will one day feel that her mother has betrayed her. She will not know the protections the women of her people have known for thousands of years. She will not know what it means to be a woman. She may ultimately be rejected even by God, and it would be better if she had never been born. So her mother will reason. And so, her mother will choose instead a little trouble in the present.

Arlene set to work stitching up the lower episiotomy. Then she had a decision to make. How completely would she repair the upper episiotomy? She knew that some in her profession would leave a more natural opening, allowing the urethra to be exposed. Arlene's colleague, Dr. Mary, would not close an upper episiotomy, claiming that to do so was tantamount to the original mutilation. Dr. Mary and Arlene both agreed that FGM was immoral. They also knew that the British had declared such acts illegal. However, the British were no longer in power and Arlene knew she had to do some repair to guard against infection. If she did not close the breach completely to its prior state, she would be interjecting her own beliefs into this woman's culture and, even worse, into this marriage's bedroom intimacies. The husband might no longer trust the wife. He might even divorce her—or, most likely, he would ask the other woman to return with her thorns and thread.

Arlene chose. She stitched the woman so she was the same as Arlene found her. The woman would need to be cut again if she bore another child.

In the dark of the early morning, Arlene packed up her midwifery bag and said her goodbyes. One of the women came toward her with a bottle in her hand. She opened the bottle. Arlene knew what was coming. The gathered women took a breath and then poured the entire bottle of perfume over Arlene's head. Ululations again filled the air. The aroma flooded the house and wafted along with Arlene through the sleeping town. She took a shower and a shampoo before collapsing into bed.

The next day, the husband sent a freshly butchered leg of lamb to the mission clinic in gratitude for the welfare of his wife and child.

In late 1961, Arlene was in Khartoum, the capital city of the Sudan. When a small Nuer church just across the Nile in the large city of Omdurman learned that Arlene was in town, they invited her to preach the sermon on Sunday. Although women did not preach in Arlene's home church in Sioux Center, she agreed to do so in Omdurman. She chose the text of Genesis 3, the chapter that begins: "Now the serpent was more subtle than any beast of the field." It is the story of the fall, when God tells the woman, "I will greatly multiply your pain in childbearing."

"Did God mean this prophecy for Eve alone, or for every woman in the pews?" asked Arlene, the preacher.

"Every woman," the congregation responded.

"Was the curse of toil and thorns for Adam alone or for every man in the pews?"

"Every man!"

"Does God mean for you to remain under this curse?"

There was murmuring, but they were not sure.

"No!" said Arlene. "He has sent you a Savior to relieve your sorrow."

"*Jeethuth!*" someone shouted.

"Yes!" said Arlene. "*Jeethuth*. God does not want the curse any more than we do. He has sent us *Jeethuth*."

"Hallelujah!" they shouted. "Amen!"

20

Do You Know Any Disciples?

*"If anyone comes to me and does not hate father
and mother, wife and children, brothers and
sisters—yes, even their own life—such a person
cannot be my disciple. And whoever does not carry
their cross and follow me cannot be my disciple.
. . . In the same way, those of you who do not give
up everything you have cannot be my disciples."*

Jesus,
Luke 14:26–27, 33 (NIV)

At two in the afternoon on Tuesday, October 15, 1963, a messenger stood at the door of Arlene's house, clapping. He held an envelope addressed to Arlene.

She opened the veranda door and received the envelope from the man's hand. The return address was the Commandant of Police. The envelope was stamped, *Strictly Confidential*. She knew what it was. She had been expecting this moment for a long time.

Back when Arlene had been in Nasir only two years, she went to a Missionary Association meeting, after which she wrote home, *They seem to think our time is limited here.*

The potential of a limited stay makes sense for foreign missions efforts. After all, the goal of missions is to provide help but also empowerment. Once the locals themselves grab hold of the mission, the missionary lets go and proceeds to another task in the same location or elsewhere.

Indeed, some local empowerment was happening at Nasir. There was now a Nuer pastor at Nasir, Moses Kuac. This one pastor, however, could not care for his small congregation and also serve as evangelist to the thousands of Nuer who migrated in and around Nasir. Moreover, Pastor Kuac's congregation could not yet pay his salary.

In the medical arena, there were Nuer dressers, but Sudanese replacements for Dr. Gordon and Arlene would be years in the future.

As for the education of the Nuer girls, Marian was a solo pioneer. She had helpers, but there was not yet any shared leadership.

Vandy was assisted by Pastor Kuac in Nuer Bible translation. Vandy and Kuac were working on not only translation but also orthography—further developing the conventions of the Nuer alphabet. Nurturing an oral language into a written language required a lengthy process of decision making, publication, literacy, and general acceptance of the linguistic choices.

All these matters would take time to transition to a full Nuer staff. Though this goal was nowhere close, the association members were already putting a time limit on their southern Sudan project. The pressure came not because the value of the missionaries was in question, but because there was a growing sense that they were no longer welcome there.

The Republic of the Sudan was young, having been born only seven years earlier in 1956. Ironically, its first civil war started before its first independence celebration: the Torit County Mutiny of August 18, 1955, had never been fully quelled. Years later, rebellious factions were growing, and there was a livelier call for not one Sudan but two.

The difficulty of communication and travel between north and south made the civil war a slow-moving phenomenon. The Mission Association members worked primarily in the south and watched the conflict from a vantage point far from the seat of power in Khartoum. The missionaries had hope that they would be able to continue despite concerns that had been building since the late 1950s.

In 1958, the northern government delivered an edict that Marian would no longer be the headmaster of the Nasir girls' school that she had started. The reason for the government's removal of Marian as a teacher was that all schooling throughout the Sudan was henceforth to be conducted in Arabic. The day after Marian heard this news, she went to the school and taught in Nuer as she had always done. Nothing changed. The edict was not enforced. It was a waiting game.

Near the end of 1958, a bloodless coup transferred power to the military. What would this mean? Would a specific plan develop for Islamic, Arabic, Khartoum-centered power? In any event, the south Sudan was short on roads, written languages, monetary systems, common culture, and media. Travel of any sort was sluggish and weather dependent. Change would not come quickly.

The following year, 1959, the army announced that they planned to occupy the Nasir mission grounds by April 15. That date came and went with no action by the local commandant or the district commissioner. These officers were often seen around the mission, but they wore friendly faces.

Late in the year, when roads were again driveable following the rainy season, army trucks began arriving. The army moved their regional headquarters next door to the mission. They put up tents and *tukls*, sandwiching the mission between the army on one side and the Arab *suk* on the other. The soldiers played their bugles bright and early. The men sprawled under the shade of the clinic trees and openly bathed on the riverfront. Arlene wrote home that she was embarrassed and disgusted. Bob wrote a series of polite complaints to the commandant and the DC, but there was no response.

Before long, the shady ground under the mission's trees was covered five times a day with Muslim prayer mats. The clinic continued to hold its own morning prayers with the patients who gathered under the large tree. Vandy held her Sunday afternoon Bible study with several dozen women who gathered under the tamarind tree close to the *suk*.

The following year, on July 27, 1960, the permanent under-secretary of the Ministry of Interior, Hassan Ali Abdullah, sent a confidential letter to the governors of the southern provinces.

> *The policy of restricting the activity of the missions in the religious sphere in order to protect the country from the danger of their success is now entering upon a decisive phase, after full inquiries on various matters and an exchange of opinions.*
>
> *I ask the governors to keep this policy secret, so that the missionaries do not learn anything of our intentions, and will thus be able to find any counter measures to our policy or to mobilize the world press and thus try to make an impression on us.*
>
> *Our officials should be very careful not to take an open stand in favour of the victory of a particular religion and they should give the appearance of supporting all in equal measure.*
>
> *The aim of these precautions is to create the right atmosphere for those responsible, so that the unanimously adopted policy can be laid down calmly and without attracting attention. Thus, it will become a fait accompli without possibility of retraction or amendment.*

The governors followed Abdullah's wishes: the secret plan was quietly followed, while religious egalitarianism remained Sudan's official public face. Abdullah's conspiracy did not come to the attention of the press until years later, after his plans regarding missionaries had been mostly accomplished.

In 1961, the Sudanese press announced that the government would take over all mission-run hospitals on July 1. Although the newspaper account was published after the supposed "takeover" date, the Nasir clinic was not taken over by the government. Once again, nothing changed.

A month later, word came that all Sudan Interior Mission (SIM) nurses from the neighboring province to the east had been expelled for reasons unknown. Next, the expulsions touched the Missionary Association to which Arlene belonged: Dottie Rankin, the missionary headmistress of the girls' school at Doleib Hill, was given seven days notice to be out of the country.

Dr. Gordon and Arlene were stunned that the SIM nurses of the Blue Nile Province had been removed. Why would the government not want its citizens to be provided with health care? The evictions of the nurses and headmistress were not known to be connected. Certainly, there were suspicions, but the permanent under-secretary's directions to act "calmly and without attracting attention" were still secret.

The uncertainties began to take a toll on Arlene's emotions. She still felt keenly the loss of her father. Her personal reserves were running low. Over the next month, she began to show signs that darkness was descending. She was becoming depressed. On August 19, 1961, she wrote, *The enemy flooding down from all sides today . . . from morning until evening. . . . He seems determined to get me down.*

She recognized that her personality came with risks, especially during unpredictable times. She copied the following from a book she was reading:

> *Typical patterns of the obsessive personality are: meticulousness, orderliness, stereotyped conduct, over conscientiousness, extreme rigidity, stubbornness . . . overprecise and self-examining with a tendency to worry and brood.*

Two weeks later, she copied this quotation from Thomas à Kempis:

> *The devil sleepeth not, neither is the flesh as yet dead; therefore cease not to prepare thyself to the battle, for on thy right hand and on thy left are enemies who never rest.*

Vandy was a true friend, but she struggled with her own melancholy. She proclaimed, "We're sitting on a rug on a highly polished floor, and the rug could be pulled out from under us any day!" Although she voiced what all of them felt, such proclamations tended to further bruise Arlene, so she sought other resources for strength and inspiration. On September 16, 1961, she copied this quotation from the great American judge, Billings Learned Hand (1872–1961):

> *The spirit of liberty is the spirit which is not too sure that it is right; the spirit of liberty is the spirit which seeks to understand the minds of other men and women; the spirit of liberty is the spirit which weighs their interest alongside its own without bias; the spirit of liberty remembers that not even a sparrow falls to earth unheeded; the spirit of liberty is the spirit of him who, near two thousand years ago, taught mankind that lesson it has never learned, but has never quite forgotten—that there may be a kingdom where the least shall be heard and considered side-by-side with the greatest.*

Learned Hand, writing from a nonreligious quarter, spoke to Arlene of a peaceable kingdom where the Nuer could live with the Arab, where there would be no northern or southern Sudan. Arlene found medicine for her soul in Learned Hand—an antidote to anything in her that leaned toward the pharisaic, perfectionist, fearful, and hopeless.

By 1962, the withering effect of the Sudan began to show in Arlene's body. She lost weight. She was incessantly tired. She was losing the strength to smile. She knew that something was wrong, but not having identified a particular ailment, she poured her energy into strengthening her spiritual disciplines. She rose earlier to pray. She studied the Scriptures. She worshiped. She spent time with fellow Christians every day. She began a personal form of the Lord's Supper, remembering his sacrifice as she privately ate a bit of bread and sipped some juice.

The government was not helping. It began to place spies everywhere. Rumor had it that the government employed informants and that many of the Nuer took the government's money. It was expected that every clinic, every worship service, every trip to the *suk* would be watched by someone and scrutinized for possible infractions. What sort of infractions? The answer to that question was largely hidden because the Sudanese government did not want the world at large to perceive them as intolerant, although one expulsion was the result of the missionary "speaking against the government." An informant testified that the missionary said, "Things are not the way they used to be."

The government's agenda came more and more into focus. The official nationwide weekly day of rest was changed to Friday, the Muslim holy day, and Qur'an studies were required in all schools.

On April 8, 1962, Arlene put a letter in the mail to Ma. The battles of her past two years were leading her somewhere, and she confessed more of her struggle than she usually did.

> *Facing things as they really are out here . . . heathenism . . . the condition of the church . . . the hopelessness of the social structure of this tribe; has a tendency to make one discouraged.*

Arlene was soft-pedaling the truth. She was worn out and living through a long, dark night. Her disciplined life of study, prayer, and Christian fellowship was calling her toward something deep and new. Her letter continued:

> *After discouragement comes depression which renders us useless. I believe we are to stand here and rejoice in spite of everything if we are to honor God in this place. What we need, too, is real disciples, not just believers. Just have begun to see the difference in studying Luke 14.*

Arlene knew that Ma would look up Jesus' strong and difficult words found in Luke 14, words that seemed to say that if Arlene didn't hate her own mother, her family, her friends Vandy and Marian, her work as a nurse, her calling to missionary service, her beloved Nasir, her life itself—if she did not forsake all these, then she could not be Christ's disciple. Arlene was trying to show Ma that the difficulties of her current circumstances began to help those strange words make more sense.

The real meaning of disciple is learner. And He wants learners who will follow Him at ANY cost. Do you know any disciples?????? I think maybe I know or have met a few . . . but they are few and far between. I am beginning to feel that unless I am willing to really be a disciple, I have no business being out here. A mere believer doesn't begin to penetrate this darkness . . . and yet I know the Lord called me out here. I don't quite understand it all . . . unless He is asking me to be a disciple. May God make me willing.

The next month Arlene was contemplating various types of weariness, identifying with F. B. Meyer's phrase, "The perpetual chafe of human sorrow." Arlene lived in a world of sorrows. In *The White Nile* by Alan Moorehead, she read about the very region in which she now nursed. The book paints a culture with "no ruins or relics of past civilizations," where "all is wild and brutal, hard, and unfeeling." The south Sudan is named as "a wilderness where life never progressed but simply turned over and over on itself in a timeless and aimless cycle." Arlene copied the above phrases into her journal, along with the following anecdote from the book.

And then Baker writes of a Nuer chief who "exhibited his wife's back and arms covered with jagged scars . . . he was quite proud of having clawed his wife like a wild beast. . . . Polygamy is, of course, the general custom; the number of a man's wives depending entirely upon his wealth, precisely as would the number of his

*horses in England. There is no such thing as love in these coun-
tries . . . everything is practical without a particle of romance.
Women are so far appreciated as they are valuable animals."*

Arlene did not herself create such severe descriptions of these
people she loved. Nevertheless, she felt a painful jolt of recognition.
Was Nuerland wild and brutal, hard and unfeeling? Yes. Did Nuer
women have the hope of being appreciated as equals to their men?
Not really. Was Nasir the capital city of perpetual human sorrow?
Definitely.

Arlene was contemplating dark mysteries of the human condition, while at the same time rejoicing in her belief that God was
good, all the time. Miraculously, she was able to embrace both
human sorrow and a good God. She had practiced living with dis-
sonance every day at the clinic as she faced birth and death, healing
and decay, comfort and pain. Arlene believed that the depth of her
contemplation was leading somewhere. Despite her terrible weariness and temptation to despair, she still had hope.

Then the Sudanese government revealed its latest treachery: the
Missionary Societies Act of 1962. The act required each missionary
to apply for a license by which they would promise, among other
things, not to "practice any social activities except within the limits
and in the manner laid down from time to time by regulations."
What was meant by "social activities" or "time to time" or "regulations" was left to the government to clarify, if and when they wished.

Interviewed by the *Sudan Daily*, an official attempted to clarify
the meaning of the act:

> *[Major-General Mohammed Nasr Osman stated], "The
> policy of the Republic of the Sudan has always been, and
> shall always be, freedom of worship for all citizens without
> discrimination."*

> *[He] also emphasized that it is equally the Government policy to combat the misuse of the freedom of worship by interference when it will endanger the harmonious security of the state.*
>
> *In this connection, the minister referred to the recent Government resolution sanctioning the deportation of a number of foreign missionaries from the Southern Sudan. "This resolution came as a result of the missionaries' proven interference in affairs outside their religious responsibilities."*

If a missionary did not apply for a license, then that person risked expulsion. Those who did apply for licenses, however, might have their applications denied for any number of arcane stipulations. Arlene was required to complete a form verifying she had not supported communists during the previous year. She filled out the form and received her license to practice as a medical missionary.

On June 13, 1962, Arlene copied into her journal a little poem by Charles Fox:

Two glad services are ours
Both the Master loves to bless
First we serve with all our powers
Then with all our feebleness.

Arlene was utterly worn out. She offered her fatigue as a gift.

At that point, the nurse became a patient. On July 4, 1962, Arlene was diagnosed with amoebic cysts, probably caused by months of dysentery and/or malaria. Her body was out of resources, and she left Nasir for two months of rest and recuperation, staying with fellow Christians in Uganda and Burundi.

During these months, Arlene recorded the following notes without attribution. The words may be from her reading, or they may be her own observations. They represent a catharsis.

> *God, who could have saved us without crosses, has not wished to do so. The operation of grace, which detaches us from ourselves and which uproots our self-love, cannot, without a miracle of grace, avoid being painful.*
>
> *God prepares a series of happenings which detaches us little by little from creatures, and at last tears us away from ourselves. Painful operation . . . painful but done in love with skill! He makes us weep. . . .*

Arlene, in her weakened body and spirit, losing hope in her own calling, was drawing closer to the One who called.

Then her days of recuperation ended. On August 27, 1962, the now thirty-eight-year-old Arlene wrote,

> *Concerning my return to Nasir . . . difficult to describe my feelings. Aware that I no longer have boundless energy, but the Lord has led me to be grateful for weakness for His strength is made perfect in weakness. Does he have some new place in mind for me? "Thine ears shall hear a word behind thee saying, 'This is the way, walk ye in it.'"*

The Thursday she arrived in Nasir, the clinic was closed but there was an emergency: a man whose arm had been bitten off by a crocodile four days earlier. Although Arlene went to work, her journal later reveals that her mind was preoccupied with the Missionary Societies Act. She was contemplating how to respond to the government's desire to limit mission workers through licensure applications. She wrote in her journal, *Our sole purpose as missionaries is to preach Jesus Christ. Let us not shy away from the whole truth of what we intend to do.*

Her meditations spilled over into the next day. She wanted to avoid the distraction of politics, and she wanted to stay focused on something larger than the Republic of the Sudan. She copied these words from an unknown source:

This life is one of continual dying. After sin-life has loosed its grip, how do we escape self-life? Back to Calvary. We must take our hands off the very blossom of our life. All things, even health, must be held loosely. Death means a loosened grasp, loosened beyond all power of grasping again. A dying must come upon all that would hinder God's working through us. May only the life of Jesus have its way in our souls.

The American mission's relationship with the Sudanese government was about to turn dire. Arlene reported, "The devil shot his missile at Akobo and Pibor. Really rocked me. Swarts and Sikkemas ordered to leave." The Swarts and Sikkemas were crucial support staff for each of those mission stations. Arlene remembered when Verne Sikkema fixed the motorboat after she and Marian had unexpectedly spent that night in the village.

Those two families prepared for their departures, and things quieted down for a few weeks. Then, on December 10, eleven missionaries of their association were given expulsion notices. Worst of all for Arlene, one of them was Vandy. The rug had been pulled out. No medical personnel were expelled. But Vandy. Van. Nyarial. Arlene felt her heart torn in half. Arlene was close to her sisters. She had many friends. But Vandy and Arlene, in these few short years, had become exceptionally close with the rare kind of heart friendship that lasts a lifetime. The south Sudan had given them to each other. Nyarial and BiGoaa. Now the north Sudan was tearing them apart.

Readers of Arlene's journals and letters will observe that by this time her thoughts constantly referenced the stories and idioms of Scripture. She didn't quote verses as proof-texts for ideas; Scripture was becoming her language. She communed with God by breathing

God's word. When she opened the Bible's pages several times a day, she resumed conversation with the God of Abraham and Sarah, Esther and Mordecai, Ruth and Naomi, Joseph and Mary, Peter and Paul.

Then there were the Psalms. Arlene's Dutch heritage included the Psalter, so she was steeped in the song collection of ancient Israel. Arlene loved hymns and choruses, but she also made a choice to keep the Psalms among the lyrics that filled her life.

Her guiding lyric for the terrible week of December 10 was Psalm 93.

> The LORD reigneth, he is clothed with majesty;
> > the LORD is clothed with strength, wherewith he hath
> > girded himself:
> > the world also is established, that it cannot be moved.
> Thy throne is established of old:
> > thou art from everlasting.
> The floods have lifted up, O LORD,
> > the floods have lifted up their voice;
> > the floods lift up their waves.
> The LORD on high is mightier than the noise of many waters,
> > yea, than the mighty waves of the sea.
> Thy testimonies are very sure:
> > holiness becometh thine house, O LORD, for ever.

Beyond her love of the words of the Psalms, it was like breathing to Arlene to sing psalms, hymns, and spiritual songs. In this aspect, she was a Nuer at heart. Even as a girl riding home from church with her father at the wheel, she was one to break into song.

> *Under His wings I am safely abiding.*
> *Though the night deepens and tempests are wild.*

It was William Cushing's nineteenth-century adaptation of Psalm 91 that Arlene sang hundreds of times throughout her life:

Still I can trust Him; I know He will keep me.
He has redeemed me, and I am His child.

By the refrain, the whole car would join in, all eight of them packed in the Pontiac, on the gravel road, crossing the railroad tracks, home to the farm, under starry Iowa skies.

Under His wings, under His wings,
Who from His love can sever?
Under His wings my soul shall abide,
Safely abide forever.

Singing was crucial during this week in 1962. Although Arlene had no one to sing with her, she still sang.

Arlene had been placed on the board of the Schutz American School, so she was in Egypt when the news of the expulsions hit. She wondered if she should go back south immediately, but she had duties there in Alexandria and therefore remained in Egypt. She went to see the pyramids.

While in Egypt, Arlene contracted malaria. She wished to be home in Nasir, but she convalesced in the north. On Christmas Day, Arlene was in Khartoum, where she picked up a copy of the *Sudan Daily*. She came upon Sudanese President Abboud's duplicitous 1962 Christmas letter.

> It gives me the greatest pleasure to offer my sincerest congratulations and best wishes, on this glorious day to you, our Christian brethren, citizens, and guests.
> The noble ideals of love and peace preached by Jesus Christ and for which he devoted and sacrificed his whole life, were designed as the best guides to world peace and stability.
> On our part, we shall give our best efforts and energies to establish these valuable ideals in our beloved Sudan.

The day after Christmas, Glenn Reed, the supervisor of the American Presbyterian Mission for the horn of Africa, arrived in Khartoum. He had come to challenge the government. This was an old story for Glenn, who had spent incalculable time haunting the offices of the Ministry of Interior. The process required that he wait for hours or even days, hoping an official would agree to speak with him in person. Now he hoped to personally appeal the numerous expulsions that had recently been announced.

Two days after Christmas, while Arlene prayed at the Khartoum mission station, Glenn went to visit the personal under-secretary of the Ministry of Interior. Although the secretary agreed to a conversation, his demeanor was hostile from the beginning.

Glenn went through the motions. "Your Excellency, may I respectfully request a reprieve or at least a postponement in the expulsion of our mission's treasurer?"

"Any good treasurer should be able to complete his calculations in six weeks time."

"He has other duties."

"Then assign his duties to another person!"

Glenn let the room fall silent. He prayed. Then he said, "May I ask a question?"

"I've answered your question concerning your treasurer."

"A separate question, Your Excellency, so that I may provide factual information to our constituents in the United States."

"One more question."

"Is there a change in the policy concerning missions in the Sudan?"

"No. Those expelled were in education, and they were no longer doing education, so their contribution to the Republic of the Sudan is complete."

"Forgive me, Your Excellency, but you have been misinformed. The persons in question were not assigned to education."

"According to our records they are in education."

"Then those records are not—"

"Those are the records on file."

"But then the files are not—"

"Perhaps in the future you should make certain you have the correct records on file."

"I'm correcting the records now."

"It's too late for these. What's the expression? Water over the dam."

"But if these people are removed, Your Excellency, their work is not the only work that will suffer. For example, the medical work will not be able to continue as it has without these support persons in place."

"That is easy. Contact the minister of health, and he will take care of it. The Sudanese government is very well coordinated!"

"All right, look, if you're expelling these so-called educators, does the expulsion of educators indicate a change in policy concerning the teaching of religion in schools?"

"No."

"What about our missionaries who have not received a response to their applications for licenses under the Missionary Act? What does this mean for them?"

"Everyone will receive an answer. Some workers will receive a license."

"And if licenses are finally approved for workers who have already been expelled, may we bring them back?"

"These particular expulsions are final."

"May we bring new workers from the States if licenses are eventually granted?"

"You will thank the government for the license but inform the office that you are unable to carry on. The appropriate offices will take that responsibility from your hands—the Department of Education, the Ministry of Health, and so on."

There was a pause. Glenn knew he had already overstayed his welcome, so he saw no harm in asking the obvious: "Does the Republic of the Sudan want us here?"

"There has been no change in our feelings toward you."

Glenn now understood what those words truly meant. He excused himself as well as he could. He stood and said, "Your Excellency."

The personal under-secretary replied, "Go in peace."

By Friday, December 28, the American Presbyterian Missionary Association of the south Sudan gathered in Malakal, and Glenn and Arlene flew in from Khartoum. The question before the association was whether to stop the work on their own schedule or wait for the government to close each station, which now seemed inevitable. Almost everyone was ready to give up and go home. Vandy argued that they should close in an orderly fashion.

Arlene was determined to stay. "We have ministry to do. To walk out and leave Nasir without any medical care, without a girls' school . . . it's not right. The people don't approve of the government's actions any more than we do." Then she added, "I might not have felt the same way six months ago, but now I'm healthy and rested. I want to stay until the Lord closes the door."

Someone said, "There are rumors of riots and fighting along the Ugandan border."

Arlene responded, "Uganda is many days from Nasir."

Glenn did not wish to be dictatorial. He went around the room and let each person decide. Bob and Vi Gordon said they would stay. Marian would stay. Everyone already knew what Arlene thought. And so, the Nasir station remained open.

Vandy, however, would not be returning. She had already said her goodbyes to the Nuer at Nasir. She would stay in Malakal and leave Africa from there.

On New Year's Day, 1963, Marian and Arlene climbed into the MAF plane at the Malakal grass strip. Arlene did not describe her parting from Vandy either in her journal or in her letters to the farm.

Arlene received strength from a letter that arrived from Elisabeth Elliot, who was working in Ecuador among the very tribe who had slain her husband. Arlene copied a portion of it into her journal:

I have ceased troubling myself about anything any more which is even days ahead. I've seen the Lord take care of things so beautifully which seemed to me impossible debacles. How often do we have to go over this lesson? Are things really in His hands, or are we the hopeless victims of men and circumstances?

Have been reading about Joseph. I can come to no other conclusion other than God intended for him to be sold into Egypt. God's purposes were accomplished through a bunch of jealous, avaricious, perfidious, pusillanimous men. Nobody lost anything by it but the sinners themselves. Joseph was imprisoned because of a lying adultress. There is no evidence that he was ever exonerated from charges which must have ruined his testimony. But the point is that no matter what men did to him, the Lord remembered him.

We, too, can count on this. He is indeed our refuge—from other men, from adverse circumstances from all that life can bring—from our very selves.

Arlene endeavored to follow Elisabeth's model. She would not trouble herself about her future in the Sudan. It seemed that her days were numbered, although she did not know how long she had. It could be a week, a month, a year, perhaps more. This truth served to heighten the importance of every day.

The year 1963 unfolded wild and brutal, full of the perpetual chafe of human sorrow, all of which served to further bind Nasir to Arlene's heart.

January

On January 24, a woman walked in from the cattle camp—the head of a fetus visible between her legs. The baby was dead.

February

On February 6, word spread through town that a five-year-old boy, Nasir Sabit, had disappeared. His clothes were found on the riverbank beside his tiny brother. Had they gone down to the river to bathe? The merchants dragged the river with a net and found nothing. It was assumed that the current had carried him downstream.

Two days later, Arlene was walking over to her house from the clinic to get a cup of coffee. She glanced toward the river. At just that moment, something under the water released its grasp, and the body of the boy rose to the surface. The current was swift, and the body headed downstream. Quickly, Arlene called for Marian. The two of them and two Nuer men climbed into the motorboat. A crowd gathered on the bank. Someone ran for the boy's family. The current pushed the body and the boat away from each other. A struggle ensued. Arlene steered the boat, attempting to come alongside. The men reached for an arm or a leg. Arlene circled. Finally someone grabbed ahold of the body. Arlene powered down the motor, and Marian tenderly slid a cloth under the boy, lifting him gently into the hull. Arlene turned the throttle and ferried the lost child toward the now wailing shore.

Arlene wrote, *Another gruesome experience but all part of a day's work in this land where life is cheap and death lurks and captures in such crude ways.*

March

This is the month the Nuer call "fire." One night, Marian and Arlene moved a card table out into the yard for supper as the outdoors offered a little more movement of air. The first rains had not yet come. The acacia tree above their table had its first two blossoms. There was a birdbath in the yard, and Arlene identified dura, bulbuls, starlings, redbreasted shrike, black and white shrike, and cordon blue. There was a hoopoe around, too.

Three days later, a *haboob* blew through. Dust and cow-dung ash blew through every crack.

April

Thɔaar, one of the mission's adult literacy teachers, stopped by to chat. He told about the time when he was a boy traveling with his family, for some reason, all the way to Khartoum. That extended trip made him a remarkable person in Nuerland, for although the Nuer are migratory, there is a region that confines their interests. Like farmers the world over, they are constrained by the needs of their animals. Thɔaar explained that his family carried a small gourd of dirt from their *kaal* because, like all Nuer, they wished to never be away from home.

Nasir had become Arlene and Marian's home. They were aware that any day could be the day they were sent to Khartoum and then beyond, never to return. One Saturday evening, they took the boat out to the middle of the river. A light haze of cattle-dung smoke hung in the moonlight over the water. They shut off the motor and drifted for a long time.

May

On Sunday, May 12, Arlene wrote in her journal the first verse of a hymn by British songwriter Frances Brook. Although two of Frances's sisters had become missionaries, her own health had stopped her:

> *My goal is God Himself, not joy, nor peace,*
> *Nor even blessing, but Himself, my God.*
> *'Tis His to lead me there, not mine, but His.*
> *At any cost, dear Lord, by any road.*

Back home in Iowa, it was planting season. Arlene had put some seeds in the Nasir ground—for lettuce, a few flowers, and some sweet corn.

On a Sunday afternoon, Arlene sat on the grass under the tamarind tree teaching the women's class. She shifted position and rose up on her knees. The woman next to her took a slight breath and pointed at the scorpion climbing on Arlene's skirt. Arlene looked down and swatted it away.

June

On Monday, June 3, the Gordon girls came running for Arlene because they saw a woman squatting in labor under the clinic tree. The delivery was completed without Arlene's help and all was well. The child was given the Nuer name *Thar Jiath*, "Under a Tree."

Things seemed to have calmed down with the government. Then one June night, Pastor Kuac's house was surrounded and he was taken into custody. The reason for his arrest seemed to be nothing other than that he was a leader in the Christian community. His arrest was a form of harassment and power play. He was locked in a cell with no bed, chair, toilet, or even a bucket. He was served bread and water. His family was allowed to bring other food, but only on Fridays.

In late June, a letter arrived from Ecuador. Vandy was there visiting Elisabeth Elliot, who had decided to move home to New Hampshire. Darkness seemed to have descended upon them both:

We've talked much about missions and whether or not we are kidding ourselves in our efforts with other people. Here as where you are one finds something of the same state of affairs in the daily routine of life. We come to the people thinking we can help them: that they need help, but our idea of what their need is does not coincide with their ideas of what they need. They, therefore, don't understand why we appeared on the scene for they fail to feel or grasp this tremendous impact that we

*think we are making. We insist they should see the love of God
from what we do, but how can they when we aren't doing what
they would have us do? We pass each other in the dark going
opposite directions. Bet [Elisabeth] is feeling more and more
the hopelessness of being a missionary.*

July

Omer came home from school. He had asked to be baptized
at the church in Omdurman where Arlene had preached her first
sermon. The church leaders in Omdurman had been uncertain
of Omer's maturity of faith, so they asked him to wait. He didn't
want to wait, so he found a Coptic priest willing to baptize him. He
had been afraid he would be kicked out of school if he was caught
writing to the missionaries in Nasir, so he hadn't written to Arlene
and Marian. Now that he was home, he spent as much time as he
dared at the mission, studying the Scriptures. He was curious about
Communion, so they studied Paul's letter to the Corinthian church:
"For as often as you eat this bread, and drink this cup, you do show
the Lord's death till he comes."

On the Friday before Omer returned to school, Marian and
Arlene took Omer to Bob and Vi Gordon's, and they all shared
Omer's first Communion.

August

Arlene spent much of the month hosting Lamberta (Lambie)
Voget, one of Vandy's professors from Wheaton College. Since
Lambie had planned this trip to Nuerland before Vandy's expulsion, she kept her plan in place. She was elderly and, unfortunately,
she experienced much back pain during her visit. Still, she went out
to speak and preach when she could and welcomed people to visit
her when she could not stand. Arlene considered her visit some
of the most enriching days of her life. Arlene served as Lambie's
interpreter, but it was Reet who gave Lambie the name *Nyarial in
Dit* (Vandy the Greater).

Late in the month, the unrest of the deep south spread north-ward, and the army instituted a curfew at Nasir. Anyone caught out between the hours of 6:00 p.m. and 6:00 a.m. would be put in prison.

September

On September 12 at the Thursday team meeting, Vi Gordon confessed her despair: "Our mission was started fifty years ago. We've been here fifty years, but what was the use? What has been the result? What do we have to show for it?"

Two weeks later, Lowrie flew to Nasir to provide updates. The real burden of his coming was to tell Arlene that her request for a reentry visa had been declined. He said there were indications that the government had something against her in their files. He recommended that she stay as long as her health was adequate. If she left the country for any reason, she would not be allowed to return. Still, he said, it seemed only a matter of time. Arlene was suddenly called away to delivery a baby. When she returned, she found Marian alone in her room, crying.

October

The rains were gone. The year was not over, but the river would be dropping soon. The messenger clapped at the veranda. Arlene took the letter from his hand. She went into the house, sat down, and opened the envelope.

21

We Will Not See Your Eyes Again

Tues. Opened clinic today with 224
patients. Bidang didn't come. A good time
at staff prayers. Talked about heaven.

October 15, 1963

The letter was quite brief:

His Excellency the Minister of Interior of the Republic of
the Sudan, in exercise of his powers under section 30(a) of the
Passports and Immigration Ordinance of 1960, has ordered the
immediate termination of your stay in the Sudan.

You are, therefore, and in compliance with the above order,
hereby given notice that you should leave the Sudan within
seven days from the 16th October 1963—on or before the 22nd
of October 1963.

M. M. Mohamedani
Commandant of Police
Upper Nile Province

Arlene sent the girl who worked at their house to run to the school and ask Marian to come home. She came and together they walked over to the Gordons and delivered the news.

The packing was accomplished in three days, with Bob fixing the clasp on Arlene's footlocker and Marian typing up the lists for customs. Each of them occasionally stopped for tears. Nuer women came and just sat, watching Arlene, looking as if someone had died. They said, "We will not see your eyes again."

After over eight years, Arlene's activities now came with an almost audible whispering, "This is the last of this." The last day at the clinic. The last time walking the path from the clinic to her house. The last prayer meeting. The last time sitting on the bench at the worship *tukl*. The final touch of each person . . . except that each person came and left and returned, again and again, to see her eyes one more time.

Marian and Arlene took the motorboat out for one last night cruise. There was no moon, but there were many mosquitos. They went home and did what they had done countless nights: read aloud to one another. At present, they were reading *Edward Wilson of the Antarctic* by George Seaver. That night they finished the book.

The next morning, the house was full of people.

Man Gaac stood up and came close to Arlene. "Nya BiGoaa. I know why you are being sent out."

"Why is that, old mother?"

"It is my fault."

"No! Old mother. Do not say such a word."

"You sat under the tree teaching us the Bible. I was there when Nyarial taught us, and then they sent her out. I told her it was my fault. I am an old fool. I never learn."

"Man Gaac, I do not know what the government thinks. But when Nyarial left, she asked me to sit with you under the tree every Sunday. If Nyarial were here, she would want it to be known that it was her fault."

Man Gaac gave the tiniest smile, made a clucking sound, and then sat down. Arlene remembered and believed what Vandy had called those Sunday Bible studies: "An hour that perhaps will be able to stand the test of eternity."

Dr. Gordon kept his chin up. "I'm sure Glenn Reed will do something so that you can return. Medical personnel are needed by this government. It's very unusual for someone in our shoes to be expelled. This is some kind of mistake."

That night, Marian cooked a final dinner for Arlene. Marian made a baked ham, but neither of the women could eat. The fridge was full of leftovers.

They slept on the riverside veranda one last time. A hyena laughed in the distance.

At first light, the golden crested cranes called out. Arlene heard it because she was already awake. She went to the clinic to see if the staff would come for prayer. They did. She spoke with them about the spiritual growth of the Christian, and Reet gave the closing prayer.

No government officials made any appearances, and their absence was a blessing. Only friends and one more round of goodbyes. Photos. Touches. Tears. A parade to the grassy airstrip. One last climb into the Cessna 57A. The closing of the door. The click of the seat belt. The whine of the prop. The acceleration, the lift, the circling, the waving, the craning of the neck. The Sobat River turned into a long snake that wriggled away through the swamps.

The route to Khartoum was through Malakal. The commandant of police met Arlene, saying that he was sorry for all this trouble and if she made an appeal at the capital, surely there would be a favorable outcome. He gave Arlene an ounce of hope.

Her plane arrived in Khartoum two days before her date to leave the country. Glenn Reed met Arlene's plane at the airport. He was leaving town and had only thirty minutes to consult about her appeal. Glenn knew well the Ministry of Interior office, having spent many hours waiting outside its door. He reminded Arlene to say, "Your Excellency." He agreed with the commandant's words, claiming he would not be surprised at all if Arlene was permitted to return to Nasir. More hope.

There was a balm waiting for her in the city: her young tutor and friend, Cieng Piŋ.

"Is it peace, my sister?"

"It is peace, my brother."

"What's this about?"

"I'm going to appeal my expulsion. Here's the letter I'm working on."

Cieng Piŋ read her letter aloud, with commentary: "*His Excellency, the Minister of Interior. The Republic* . . . blah, blah, blah, *Your Excellency* . . . *I assume I must be considered a security risk—*" He looked at Arlene. "You? *You?*"

He read on:"*Because I have due respect for the authorities who have the responsibility of maintaining law and order, and because it is still my desire to serve the welfare of the Sudan and her people, I hereby appeal to Your Excellency for review of whatever charge may be against me. . . . In the event that Your Excellency—*Nyarial would be scoffing at all these 'Excellencies.'"

"If they work, I'll be the one laughing."

"If God does not work, neither can we."

"You have been a good brother to me, Cieng Piŋ."

"My sister, no matter what, you will be back."

"Or I will see you somewhere else."

"*E jen* [It is good]."

"*E jen pany* [It is very good]."

When the office of the Ministry of the Interior opened at 9:00 a.m. on Monday, Arlene was there to hand over her letter of appeal. The secretary of the permanent under-secretary took Arlene's letter and walked into the inner office. Arlene sat and waited. Eventually an assistant secretary to the secretary of the permanent under-secretary handed Arlene a piece of paper that read: *Wednesday, October 23, Noon.*

Arlene responded, "But your office has required me to be out of the country tomorrow, Tuesday, October 22."

The assistant secretary observed, "Clearly, His Excellency has changed his mind."

Arlene rejoiced that the permanent under-secretary was allowed to change his mind. More hope.

Elsewhere in Khartoum, who should show up that day at the mission where Arlene was staying? Omer. The grapevine had reached him. He came to declare his own certain hope that Arlene would be allowed to stay.

The next day was Tuesday, waiting day. Arlene's journal acknowledges that her heart was "filled with fear at the thought of standing before authorities tomorrow." Arlene was always calm in the clinic and operating room, even though the stakes were life and death. But her knees buckled in the arena of public argument. She remembered and wrote in her journal the encouragement Jesus gave to his first disciples:

> *You will be brought before kings and governors for my name's sake. This will be a time for you to bear testimony.*

Wednesday arrived. Omer came early to pray. Then Arlene was driven across the large city on dusty roads. The dust and sand filtered everywhere—into the car, her hair, and her eyes. She was glad she was not a woman who wore makeup. Arriving at the government compound, she wound her way to the P.U.-S.'s office and made her presence known. Her appointment was for noon. Like any Schuiteman, Arlene was early. She was offered tea as an expression of Arabic hospitality. Arlene drank it as a courtesy. The cup was kept full, and she kept sipping.

Arlene had wandered into a man's world. There was one public restroom, off the central courtyard, large and open, with several holes in the ground. Shortly before noon, Arlene faced a common human predicament that threatened to make her miss her appointment. What could she do except admit her predicament to a man? The stranger was a gentleman and stood guard at the restroom door, a small act of graciousness as the clock struck twelve. Arlene returned to the office. "No thank you." She didn't want more tea. Suddenly—

"Miss Schuiteman? His Excellency will see you now."

Arlene entered a large room with one large desk. She quickly took in what seemed to her a somewhat graceless, bureaucratic environment. Straight ahead was a wall of metal filing cabinets. At one side of the room were uncurtained windows with shutters that could be closed in the event of a *haboob*. Straw mats covered the floor. Overhead hung a single bulb. There was the rhythmic hum of a fan. Behind the large desk sat Hassan Ali Abdullah, the permanent under-secretary himself. He pointed to a small metal chair in front of his desk. Arlene sat down.

The P.U.-S. did not stand or shake hands. He had a file folder on the desk in front of him. Arlene waited for him to speak first, as Glenn Reed had instructed her.

"I trust Khartoum has been treating you well, Miss Schuiteman."

"Yes, Your Excellency. Thank you for seeing me on such short notice, Your Excellency."

"I have reviewed your file. What are you hoping for today?"

"I wish to review whatever charges may be against me."

"Well, that is easy. There is no case against you that can be defended in court, so no charges will be brought." The P.U.-S. picked up the file folder in front of him and flung it into a tray at the edge of his desk.

Arlene was stunned. "No charge?"

"You have understood completely."

"So I will not be expelled from the country?"

"Please, I thought you had understood. Your termination is without possibility of retraction. But you will not be charged in the courts."

"This is a very strange procedure. Not being allowed to answer an accusation."

"If there were an accusation, it would be tried in the courts, not here."

"Must I tell my people that I was asked to leave without a reason given?"

"Tell them whatever you like. Now kindly excuse me." Then the P.U.-S. gestured toward the door.

Arlene sent a cablegram to Glenn Reed: *NO SOAP COMING SUNDAY.*

Her coded message meant that the attempt to clean up this mess had been unsuccessful. Arlene would be flying out of the Sudan the following Sunday.

Arlene also sent a cable to Marian back in Nasir: *PROV 16:33.* Marian would understand the reference to the biblical verse in Proverbs, "Into the lap the lot is cast, and the final disposition is the Lord's." Arlene and Marian adhered to a higher authority than the P.U.-S. of the Republic. Arlene added, *TELL WOMEN MY HEART UNDER TREE WITH THEM EACH SUNDAY.*

Since the government was interested in saving face with the world community, especially the United States, it released a statement to the Sudanese press. Arlene Schuiteman was among the blacklisted, because her "activities are aimed at destroying the unity between the North and the South, and she taught that Christianity was the cure for all their ills."

After listening to the Sudanese grapevine, Lowrie and Glenn learned the following story. One day in 1963, a woman of the village had come to Arlene with symptoms that, upon examination, presented as venereal disease. The woman confessed that she was having an extramarital affair with an army officer in Nasir. She was his mistress. Arlene consistently seized every opportunity to address not only disease but also disease prevention. She cautioned the woman against further contact with the officer for health reasons and because the practice was against Arab, Nuer, Islamic, and Christian moral standards. Arlene's counsel apparently influenced the woman because she told the officer she would no longer see him. When he asked her why, she said that the missionary nurse told her not to. That was how Arlene had eroded the "unity between the North and the South," the officer being from the North and his village mistress being from the South. The officer was upset and sent his desire for reprisal up the chain of command.

Although the government officials' stated reason for blacklisting Arlene had a whisper of truth in it, they were also guarding a secret so nefarious they could hardly even admit it to themselves. The truth was that the government did not want missionaries to provide medical care for the southern Sudan because they did not wish *anyone* to provide medical care for the southern Sudan. They were desirous that the black, animistic, tribal southerners would die. Their idea was to solve the medical needs of the south through attrition. Arlene and her kind were standing in the way. The Sudanese government was, after all, very well coordinated on this matter.

The Sudanese government's position was that Arlene, a thirty-nine-year-old missionary nurse, was a revolutionary. Although she claimed she was not a revolutionary, she was nevertheless expelled. She had spent more than eight years nursing the tribe Tom Lambie had doctored, living on the same plot of land where Tom had pounded in the tent pegs for his first riverside clinic.

Arlene flew to the Holy Land. In the dusty countryside south of Bethlehem, she visited Tom Lambie's widow. Irma still lived at the tuberculosis sanatorium she had founded with her husband. Mrs. Lambie asked Arlene, "Where will you go next?"

Arlene did not know. She had been told about an immediate need for nurses in Ethiopia. Earlier in her life, the evidence of need would have been nearly enough for her to go. Now she answered Mrs. Lambie, "I've been told they need a nurse in Ethiopia, but I want to know the Lord's will for me. One does not determine that solely by seeing need."

Mrs. Lambie smiled and nodded. She knew the process, but she remarked, "If you ever do get to Ethiopia, ask about the evangelist Gidada. They say he's memorized the entire Bible. He lives in Dembi Dollo. He's old now, like me."

On November 22, 1963, while Arlene was visiting in Bethlehem, a shot rang out in Dallas, Texas. The 35th President of the United States, John F. Kennedy, was riding in a convertible, waving to the crowds. The bullet struck him in the head, killing him instantly. The whole world gasped. Probably some of the Nuer ran to the forest. The world was suddenly so small that memorial observances for the American president were held around the globe. Arlene attended the service in Jerusalem. Then she went home to Iowa.

22

The Sobat River Overflows

*Now that I am old and gray, do not
abandon me, O God. Let me proclaim your
power to this new generation, your mighty
miracles to all who come after me.*

Psalm 71:18 (NLT)

Lime, lime, lime gwa Kuoth thin.
[It is a sweet place. God is there.]
Ba ne rom nee ciang kel, nee ciang kel.
[We will meet one day, one day.]

Vandy's Nuer version of the hymn
"In the Sweet By and By"

Soon after Arlene departed from the Sobat River, the slaying began and genocide bled into what would become decades of civil war.

The news from the Sudan sickened Arlene, and she and Vandy wept over the phone. Even as they supported each other, they lost track of Sudanese friends who either were dead or had fled. This became the era of "the lost boys" of the Sudan.

Arlene eventually returned to Africa—to Ethiopia and Zambia—but never Nasir. Neither Arlene nor Vandy ever set foot again in the Sudan.

In 1989, Arlene retired to Sioux Center, Iowa. She moved in with her sister, Grada, into the tan brick, one-story house Ma and Pa had built on 2nd Avenue, a few houses north of the Christian school. Grada was seven years younger than Arlene, and like Arlene, had never married. Having moved off the farm with Ma and Pa, she had cared for Ma through Pa's sudden death and Ma's struggle with Alzheimer's disease. Arlene took a bedroom on the main floor, at the other end of the hall from Grada, who was thrilled to have her sister home for good.

As it turned out, Arlene was not the only ex-Sudan resident to arrive in the Midwest. Thousands of boys, and then girls, and finally whole families managed to flee across the African continent and then across the Atlantic. Many eventually gathered in immigrant communities in the heartland of the United States. Like the Dutch of northwest Iowa, they moved near to those who shared their language and culture. They started over, holding little hope of ever returning home.

One of the Sudanese refugee streams happened to flow into Sioux Falls, South Dakota, an hour and a half drive from Arlene's door. By the early 1990s, when Osama Bin-Laden was setting up headquarters in Khartoum, the refugee numbers in Sioux Falls grew into the thousands.

One night, a woman's screams pierced the quiet of a Sioux Falls neighborhood. There was shouting and the thwack of a fist, or a belt, or a board. The horrendous sounds carried on until someone finally called the police.

A squad car swept onto the scene with flashing lights and siren. Men in blue charged up the stairs and, before long, escorted the suspect out of the house in handcuffs. He was a black man with six scars lined neatly across his forehead. A disheveled black woman followed behind, wailing in protest. Even though she was not speaking English, it was clear that she was saying, "Don't, don't, don't take my man from me!" The police officers ignored her. They knew the familiar story of a battered woman who immediately came to her lover's defense. They knew that if they did not act now, the next time they might be carrying out a body bag. The officers pushed the woman aside and put the man in the car.

The news spread within the Nuer community. Someone ob-
tained a lawyer, and the lawyer talked to the man in custody. The
lawyer then asked around, trying to get to the truth of the matter.
Someone gave him a phone number across the Big Sioux River
in Iowa.

Arlene and Grada were sitting in twin La-Z-Boy recliners in
their quiet living room when the phone on the little table between
them rang. Grada answered it and then handed the phone to Arlene.

A voice asked, "Is this Arlene Schuiteman?"

"Yes, this is Arlene."

"I'm a lawyer in Sioux Falls. I have a client who's in jail. He's
Nuer. I understand you know the Nuer."

"Yes."

"You know their language?"

"Some. It's been a long time."

"And you know their culture?"

"Yes. What's the man's name?"

"I can't tell you that just yet, but I have a question. Are Nuer men
expected in their culture to beat their wives?"

Arlene paused at that. There was no good answer. "Some Nuer
believe that a man should do that—that if a husband loves his wife,
he will discipline her. They believe that the other women will talk
if he doesn't. If a wife is not beaten from time to time, the other
women will say her husband doesn't notice her anymore, doesn't
care anymore, maybe even doesn't want her around anymore."

"Is that what you believe?"

"No. I believe that a husband and wife should love each other
and never harm each other. I've known Nuer men who changed
their beliefs about beating their wives. But these things run deep.
May I speak with this man?"

"May I call you back?"

"I'd like that."

The lawyer never called again, and Arlene never found out what
happened, though she began making calls of her own. She discovered

that Nuer were settling in various sections of Sioux Falls. In each neighborhood, they located a church and asked permission to use the sanctuary once a month on a Sunday afternoon. This was a welcome arrangement. Arlene discovered six Nuer congregations and in 1997 began visiting them one by one. She would attend worship in Sioux Center on Sunday morning, pack a sandwich for the road, make the hour and a half drive in her red Ford Taurus, attend an hours-long Nuer service, and then make the drive back to Sioux Center in time for the evening service at First Reformed. Since the Nuer congregations scheduled their meetings with African flexibility, it took Arlene many months to get around to each of them even once.

Almost precisely forty-three years after Arlene and Vandy trekked out in the Jeep to find Yuɔl, Arlene drove to Sioux Falls for an afternoon Nuer worship service at St. Mark's Lutheran Church. Located in the heart of Sioux Falls, this church has an unusual worship center that seems to be all roof, with four sides sloping almost to the ground, looking like a grand *tukl*. Arlene had worshiped with this Nuer congregation before, but on this particular day there was a guest preacher—a female evangelist who had not met Arlene and was perhaps not used to seeing a white woman in the congregation. After her sermon, the evangelist looked at Arlene and asked her, in English, "And would you please tell us who you are?"

Arlene was a bit surprised at the question. She wondered if the question was hospitality or was actually masking a guarded suspicion. After suffering from years of harm brought by strangers from outside their tribes, the Sudanese had earned the right to be suspicious. Knowing this, Arlene stood and answered the guest preacher's question in English, "I am Arlene Schuiteman of Sioux Center, Iowa." Then she continued in Nuer, "*E an Nya BiGoaa Jon ka Nasir* [But really, I am Nya BiGoaa Jon from Nasir]."

There was loud applause. The evangelist smiled and nodded, and then she brought the service to a close.

Unbeknownst to Arlene, there was another special guest visiting that day—a young man who was attending the university an hour away in Vermillion. As the service broke up, he approached Arlene.

"Nya BiGoaa? I think you knew my father."

"Who's your father?"

"My father was Cieng Piŋ Luak."

Arlene felt as if time stood still. She thought that she might faint. She did not speak.

The young man continued, "I am Khor, son of Cieng Piŋ."

Arlene finally spoke, "*Mal mi goaa*, Khor?"

"It is peace, Nya BiGoaa. My father was your friend."

"He taught me your language." Arlene wagged her head, still coming to grips with the truth right in front of her. "Khor, son of Cieng Piŋ."

Khor grinned and nodded.

Arlene asked, "Do you have other family here?"

"My wife Rosanna is here. She's from the Dinka people. I paid a hundred cows for her. We had a beautiful wedding for many days. I don't speak Dinka, but she knows Arabic. I translate now for the United States government. Our children are named Virginia, where Rosanna and I got married, and little Cieng Piŋ. I don't know if you knew my great uncle Yuɔl."

"Oh yes!"

"Many of his family became Christians. Some of them are here in the United States. His son Choel is a pastor in Minneapolis."

Tears welled in Arlene's eyes, making it difficult to maintain her smile, but she had another important question. She had learned years before that Khor's father had succumbed to tuberculosis, but what of Khor's mother—was she alive?

Khor nodded, "She is in the Sudan. We are hoping to bring her soon."

"You will, Khor."

"God will. If God does not work, we can do nothing."

"*Awhn.*"

"Yes."

That night, Arlene wrote in her journal, *My joy leaped up within me. After all these years!*

So it happened that the Sobat River rose and flowed through Arlene's Iowa living room. There was Khor and Rosanna with their children, Virginia and Cieng Piŋ. And the baby, whose name, they proudly announced, was Nya BiGoaa Khor. Arlene reached out her large, ancient hands, and Rosanna placed the tiny namesake into her arms. The two BiGoaas stared at each other—one looking up and the other looking down—making sounds that needed no translation.

Then came Easter weekend of Arlene's eightieth year. She stood on her veranda, watching a throng of Nuer climbing out of a car in front of her house. There were children and adults and one older woman. Arlene laughed and clapped her hands. Man Juba, Cieng Piŋ's widow, was walking up Arlene's Sioux Center driveway. The doorway Pa had built wide enough for a coffin to be carried out was now full of jubilant Nuer flooding in.

Man Juba took Arlene's hands. "*Mal mi goaa, Nya BiGoaa Jon* [Is it peace, Miss You-Will-Be-Good, Daughter-of-John]?"

"*Awhn, mal e* [Yes, peace]."

Man Juba lifted her eyes heavenward and began to pray in fluid, passionate Nuer, "Old Father, we call you now, we the people of sin. You, Chief, help us. You are the one with power. Let your heart be soft."

The living room repeated, "Let your heart be soft!" Arlene joined their voices, the language returning with miraculous ease.

Man Juba shouted, "We are praising you now!"

The room agreed, "We are your praisers!"

Man Juba called out, "What has God done?!"

The room responded, "What has God done?!"

Man Juba ended her prayer, "We are calling you with the name of your son, *Jeebuth*."

The little brick house on 2nd Avenue confirmed, "*Inono!*" Amen and amen.

Arlene wondered for a moment if this very day was what God had intended all along. Then she told herself that such gifts cannot be fully understood and must simply be received, for as Vandy had professed to her, "Only God knows what Jesus meant when he said to go and make disciples."

✹ Selected Bibliography

"Anxiety in the Sudan." *The Tablet*, December 1, 1962.

Baillie, John. *A Diary of Private Prayer*. New York: Charles Scribner's Sons, 1949.

Balisky, E. Paul. "Lambie, Thomas Alexander." *Dictionary of African Christian Biography*. http://www.dacb.org/stories/ethiopia/lambie-thomas3.html.

Barker, Jeff. *Arlene: An African Trilogy*. Play presented by Northwestern College Theatre Department, Orange City, Iowa, 2014.

———. *Iowa Ethiopia*. Play presented by Northwestern College Theatre Department in the United States and Ethiopia, 2011–12.

———. *Sioux Center Sudan*. Play presented by Northwestern College Theatre Department in North America and Japan, 2006–10.

———. *The Storytelling Church: Adventures in Reclaiming the Role of Story in Worship*. Cleveland, TN: Webber Institute Books, 2011.

———. *Zambia Home*. Play presented by Northwestern College Theatre Department in North America, 2013.

Barnes-Dean, Virginia Lee. "Clitoridectomy and Infibulation." *Cultural Survival Quarterly* 9, no. 2 (Summer 1985).

Bulpett, C. W. L. *A Picnic Party in Wildest Africa: Being a Sketch of a Winter's Trip to Some of the Unknown Waters of the Upper Nile*. London: Edward Arnold, 1907.

Churchill, Winston. *The River War: An Account of the Reconquest of the Sudan*. London: Longmans, Green, and Co., 1899.

Deng, Francis M. "Sudan—Civil War and Genocide: Disappearing Christians of the Middle East." *Middle East Quarterly* 8, no. 1 (Winter 2001): 13–21.

Dirie, Waris. *Desert Flower: The Extraordinary Journey of a Desert Nomad*. New York: HarperCollins, 1998.

"Ecuador: Mission to the Aucas (The Hemisphere)." *Time*, January 1956, 30.

Elliot, Elisabeth. "The Prayer of the Five Widows." *Christianity Today*, January 1957.

Gordon, Bob, and Vi Gordon. "Memoirs and Letters." Unpublished manuscript, 2002.

Harris, Hilary (co-director and producer) and George Breidenbach (co-director). *The Nuer*. Film. Cambridge, MA: Harvard University, The Film Study Center of the Peabody Museum, 1971.

Hudson, David, Marvin Bergman, and Loren Horton. *The Biographical Dictionary of Iowa*. Iowa City: University of Iowa Press, 2009.

Killmer, Joyce. *Trees and Other Poems*. New York: George H. Doran, 1914.

Lambie, Thomas A. *A Doctor's Great Commission*. Wheaton, IL: Van Kampen, 1954.

———. *Doctor without a Country*. New York: Fleming H. Revell, 1939.

Langley, Michael. *No Woman's Country: Travels in the Anglo-Egyptian Sudan*. New York: Philosophical Library, 1951.

Lewis, C. S. *The Four Loves*. Northern Ireland: Geoffrey Bles, 1960.

———. *Mere Christianity*. United Kingdom: Geoffrey Bles, 1952.

———. *The Problem of Pain*. United Kingdom: The Centenary Press, 1940.

———. *Surprised by Joy*. United Kingdom: Geoffrey Bles, 1955.

Moorehead, Alan. *The White Nile*. New York: Harper & Brothers, 1960.

Nightingale, Florence. *Notes on Nursing*. New York: D. Appleton and Company, 1860.

Ratmeyer, Una. *Hands, Hearts, and Voices: Women Who Followed God's Call*. New York: Reformed Church, 1995.

Ruay, Deng D. Akol. *The Politics of Two Sudans: The South and the North, 1821–1969*. Uppsala, Sweden: Nordiska Afrikainstitutet, 1994.

Salon, Gidada. *The Other Side of Darkness*. New York: Friendship, 1972.

Shields, Ried F. *Behind the Garden of Allah*. Philadelphia: United Presbyterian Board of Foreign Missions, 1937.

Svoboda, Teresa, trans. *Cleaned the Crocodile's Teeth: Nuer Song*. Greenfield Center, NY: The Greenfield Review, 1985.

Swart, J. Robert. "It's Sort of Like Dying." *The Church Herald*, July 1961, 11.

Swart, Morrell F. *The Call of Africa: The Reformed Church in America Mission in the Sub-Sahara, 1948–1998*. Historical Series of the Reformed Church in America. Grand Rapids: Eerdmans, 1998.

Vandevort, Eleanor. *A Leopard Tamed*. New York: Harper and Row, 1968. Reprinted with new foreword and introduction. Peabody, MA: Hendrickson, 2018.

———. "Pedagogical Grammar of Nuer." *Nuer Field Notes*. http://www.dlib.indiana.edu/collections/nuer/index.html.

"World: The Sudan." *Time*, July 1965.

The Schuiteman sisters (clockwise): Harriet (tallest), Bernice, Arlene (holding Milly), Joyce, and Grada (1937).

JANUARY 1

1943 *Friday* - Grandma Schuiteman's 69th birthday. Went out there in P.M. Lots of fun. Cold and icy so we had to stay home at night.

1944 *Saturday* - Went to Grandma S. for dinner. Played Banaza. Cort & Johann here for supper.

1945 *Monday* - Went to Grandma S. in P.M. Nelvina there, too. Played Snap, etc. Stayed home at night.

1946 *Tuesday* - Grandpa S still very sick. Very bad itch all over body. Grandma 72nd birthday. Xmas program in P.M. (postponed because of snow) Mamma home overnight

1947 *Wednesday* - Didn't go to church in A.M. but worked on program material. Pete & Gladys here in P.M. Minn & Ed here for supper.

The first page of Arlene's first journal.

Arlene as country school teacher at Plato Township School #2 (around 1943).

Students of Plato Township School #2, Sioux County, Iowa (around 1943).

Graduation from the Methodist Hospital School of Nursing, Sioux City (1954).

Ma and Pa Schuiteman agree to a photo with Arlene's new Argos C3 (December 1954).

A steamboat on the Sobat River (1955).

Tukls at evening in the village of Kuanylualthoaan across the river from Nasir.

The two *tukls* of a farmer's wives on either side of his barn.

Cattle are at the center of Nuer life.

Missionary Aviation Fellowship's 57A Cessna landing at flat-as-a-pancake Nasir.

Water carrying at sunrise.

Patients receiving initial diagnoses in the shade of the clinic tree at Nasir.

Fishing Day (1955).

A frightened girl clutches Arlene during Fishing Day (1955).

Arlene and Nuer at "the place of magic" (the Nasir Clinic) on the Sobat River.

Marian Farquhar had a passion for education. She spent her breaks traveling to outlying areas to teach children who did not attend the boarding school at Nasir.

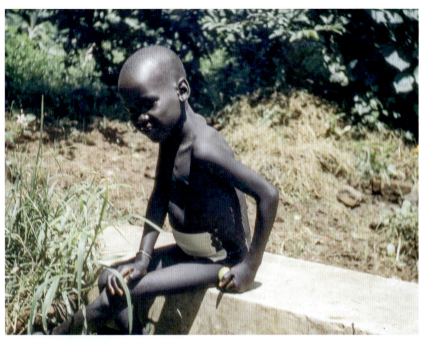

Jɔk Jak, the brave boy who survived the encounter with a cow's horn (1956).

Arlene with Jɔk Jak (1956).

The linguist (Eleanor Vandevort), the teacher (Marian Farquhar), and the nurse (Arlene) with Dr. Gordon's son, Johnny (1960).

Kɔŋ and Yuɔl talking about *Jeethuth* (*Jeebuth*) with Cieng Piŋ (1957).

Yuɔl departs Nasir for his home village of Pi Jiaak (1957).

Teenagers examining the Jeep (1957).

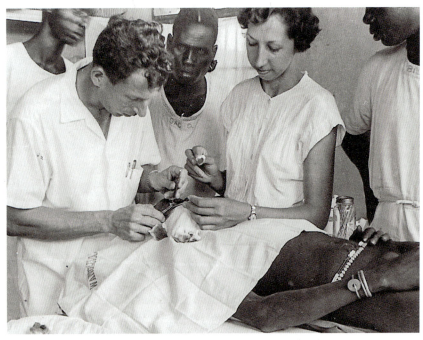

Arlene assisting Dr. Gordon in surgery at Nasir (1961).

First Reformed Church, Sioux Center, Iowa (2006).
Kneeling in front: Sarah Kuac (daughter of Pastor Kuac Nyoat).
Sitting (from left to right): Dr. Bob Gordon, Eleanor Vandevort, Arlene Schuiteman,
Bafal Gat Deang, and Man Juba. Standing: Jeff Barker and his Northwestern drama
students and Sudanese guests, some of whom traveled long distances to be present.

Arlene and Jeff Barker at Arlene's home in Sioux Center, Iowa (2017).